PENGUIN HANDBOOKS

THE WINES OF GERMANY

Cyril Ray, born in 1908, was a scholar both of Manchester Grammar School and of Jesus College, Oxford. He has been a war correspondent, a foreign correspondent, and a UNESCO special commissioner in various European and African countries. He has been 'Atticus' of the *Sunday Times*, assistant editor of the *Spectator*, and author of military histories, but is best-known as a writer on wine.

In 1965, Cyril Ray received the Wine and Food Society's first André Simon Award for his services to gastronomic literature and especially for his editorship of the then annual anthology, *The Compleat Imbiber*. In 1967, with the publication of *The Wines of Italy* (in Penguin Books), which was translated into Italian, he became the first Englishman to be awarded Italy's similar prize, the Bologna Trophy.

Founder, now President, of the Circle of Wine Writers, Cyril Ray has been honoured by the Italian and the French governments for his contributions to the literature of wine: he is a Cavaliere dell' Ordine al Merito della Repubblica Italiana and a Chevalier du Mérite Agricole.

He recently collaborated with his wife, Elizabeth – cookery correspondent of the *Observer* and editor of *The Best of Eliza Acton*, which is in Penguin Books – in a light-hearted work of pooled knowledge and experience, *Wine with Food*. Cyril Ray's most recent publications include *The Wines of France* and *The Wines of Germany*.

THE
WINES
OF
GERMANY

*

CYRIL RAY

PENGUIN BOOKS

Penguin Books Ltd, Harmondsworth, Middlesex, England
Penguin Books, 625 Madison Avenue, New York, New York 10022, U.S.A.
Penguin Books Australia Ltd, Ringwood, Victoria, Australia
Penguin Books Canada Ltd, 2801 John Street, Markham, Ontario, Canada L3R 1B4
Penguin Books (N.Z.) Ltd, 182–190 Wairau Road, Auckland 10, New Zealand

First published by Allen Lane 1977
Published in Penguin Books 1979

Made and printed in Great Britain by
Richard Clay (The Chaucer Press) Ltd,
Bungay, Suffolk
Set in Monotype Bembo

For
my old friend
and fellow-traveller
through Europe's vineyards
REGGIE PECK

Contents

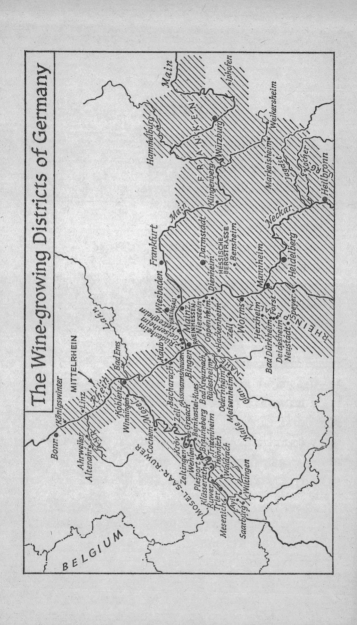

The Wine-growing Districts of Germany

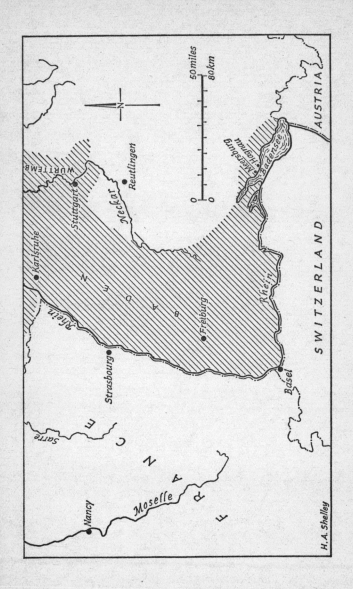

AUSTRIA

SWITZERLAND

50 miles
80 km

N

WÜRTEMB

Reutlingen

Stuttgart

Neckar

Karlsruhe

Rhein

B A D E N

Freiburg

Rhein

Überlingen
Meersburg
Bodensee

Basel

Strasbourg

Sarre

F R A N C E

Moselle

Nancy

H. A. Shelley

Introduction

After I had written and had had published books about the wines of Italy and the wines of France it was to be expected that I should be asked to write a similar guide – though introduction would be the better word – to the wines of Germany.

This time I was more diffident.

Although I had first visited German vineyards – specifically, that is, to see the vineyards as such, and not merely in the course of a trip to Germany – as long ago as 1952, and had renewed my acquaintance with them often enough since; although I had drunk more different German wines at home since the war than usually come the way of people outside the wine trade, and had frequently written about them in the public prints – nevertheless, I felt myself to be far less knowledgeable about them than about French and Italian wines.

Partly, it was – and is – a matter of language.

Imperfect though my knowledge is of French and of Italian, I had a smattering of each, enough to feel reasonably at home and at ease in either country – to fumble through a newspaper, to ask my way, to order a meal, and to talk, however haltingly and with however vile an accent, to those wine-growers and wine-shippers who had no English.

Not so in Germany. How often in the last half-century have I wished that I had listened to my grandparents speaking Yiddish, and that they had lived long enough for me to have picked up at any rate that dialect of German! But no, and because I had, and have, no German I have never felt completely at my ease in Germany; and its way of life, therefore – which includes, of course, its way with wine – has seemed to be always that one degree less easy to understand than the ways of its neighbours south of the Alps and west of the Rhine.

Easy enough, of course, to master the key words of the German wine-list – to know why an *Auslese* is likely to be sweeter, and certain to be dearer, than a *Spätlese*, and to distinguish between a *trocken* wine, at one end of the scale of sweetness, and a *Trockenbeerenauslese*, at the other.

Anything more subtle, though, has taken more time and harder work to master, and much waited to be revealed to me until my latest long journey through all the wine-growing regions of Germany, in the autumn of 1975, during which this book was finished, in the company of the old friend to whom it is dedicated, bilingual in English and German, and an enthusiastic amateur of wine.

*

Another barrier to complete understanding has been the wines themselves.

In their own country, as I shall show later, they are mostly drunk, and mostly made to be drunk, not with meals but between them and after them, which is not the English way.

Here, wine is considered as to be drunk with meals, and usually the main course of a meal decides what wine shall be drunk with it. As main courses here are more frequently of meat than of fish; as the British tradition is to drink red wine with meat; and as virtually all German wines are white – few German reds exist, and fewer still come to this country – hocks and Mosels are drunk less frequently than clarets and burgundies.

Then again, although as I shall show later there is a deeply rooted hock-drinking tradition in this country, there are many devoted lovers of German wines who nevertheless consider them too fragrant and flowery to go with fish dishes, with which they prefer the drier wines of Alsace, Burgundy or the Loire.

They love hocks and Mosels dearly, but they do not drink them so often, and what is not drunk so often is not talked about so much.

(It may be that in time we shall see here more of the wines of Franconia, Württemberg and Baden, which are drier than the familiar wines of the more northerly regions, in which case the dry French whites will be given a run for their money.)

Meanwhile, I have drunk and discussed good hocks and Mosels in England with those who are knowledgeable about them – but nothing like so much or so often as good clarets and burgundies. If only Piesporter had come my way as frequently as port!

What is more, different though they can be, and are, from each other, there is a far greater family resemblance between all German wines than between all French or all Italian wines.

No two German red wines differ so widely, say, as a great Hermitage and a fine claret: not even a Franconian Silvaner and a Rheingau Riesling are so different as a white burgundy and a white Bordeaux. Again, this means less to ponder over, less to talk about.

And yet, when this opportunity arose to cast my mind back to those German wines I had tasted in the past, to what I had been taught about them and what I had written about them; to taste others now and consider them more carefully; to revisit Germany more purposefully and to marshal my thoughts about its vineyards and its wines; it seemed one not to be missed.

I learned a great deal by undertaking this book: I would not make so bold as to express the hope that it will also teach others a great deal – only that it will help them towards learning more for themselves about the wines of Germany. They are worth knowing.

*

In my Penguin book on the wines of Italy I listed every Italian wine the name of which I knew to be in any way officially or (because the official lists are still far from complete) even generally recognized; in the companion book on the wines of France I listed all those entitled by French law to an *appellation contrôlée*, or to bear the seal denoting a *vin délimité de qualité supérieure*.

Here, for the sake of uniformity with these other books, I list under each region the vineyards listed individually in the official Weinbergsrolle, or register of vineyards, required by the German wine law.

As there are more than 3,000 of them, however, and as within each region the individual wines differ so little, it is impossible to comment on each individually, as I came near to doing in the other books.

I had intended – and had indeed begun – to mark those that I and others had found to be of especially high quality. Even this, though, proved invidious. It is truer of German wines than of others that so much depends on the vintage year, and on the state of ripeness of the grapes at vintage time, that it is impossible to say that this wine is worthy of a mark and that one not; that it is true of the 1970s but not of the 1975s; of the *Spätlese*, but not of the *Auslese*; of this owner's part of the named vineyard, but not of that.

The only advice I can give is to seek guidance from wine-merchants in Britain and from growers and shippers in Germany. Then, to make comparative tastings when possible and, after that, to drink what is most pleasing. To be more specific I should have to be less judicious.

A major difficulty in compiling these lists has been that of all the eleven specific regions (*Anbaugebiete*) nine are divided into anything between two and seven *Bereiche*, or sub-regions; each of these in turn into *Grosslagen*, or greater sites; these into the individually named vineyards (*Einzellagen*), which are grouped in all lists not alphabetically but under their respective villages.[1]

There is no way that I, or anyone else, has been able to discover by which a single vineyard can be found in its own alphabetical place under the name of its region.

Nor are the *Bereiche* or the *Grosslagen* or the villages in alphabetical order. The lists give the *Bereiche* not alphabetically but in geographical order, some from north to south, some south to north, with the villages similarly disposed, and so, too, the vineyards within the villages, numbered to match numbers on closely detailed maps.

The system I have devised here, as being the simplest I can, is based to some extent on that of Alexis Lichine in the new and revised edition of his great reference work,[2] which by happy chance appeared as I was finishing this book.

So far as I can see, he lists the *Bereiche* arbitrarily, in some cases alphabetically, in some geographically, as in the official publications. These I have rearranged alphabetically.

Under these he has listed the *Grosslagen* apparently as arbitrarily, and I have rearranged these, too.

---

1. 'The *bestimmtes Anbaugebiet* is a designated region carrying the official name of each of the eleven German wine-producing areas. Each of these largest regions is divided into one or more sub-regions, or districts, called a *Bereich*. Within the *Bereich* are found the separate villages and the vineyards associated with them. These towns or communes may be variously called *Weinbauort*, *Gemeinde*, or *Gemarkung*. As for the vineyards themselves, an individual plot is called an *Einzellage*, but all of the *Einzellagen* are officially grouped into sections of vineyards named *Grosslagen*.' Lichine, Alexis, *Encyclopaedia of Wines and Spirits*, London, Cassell, 1975.

2. Lichine, Alexis, op. cit.

But I am grateful to him for having at any rate listed the villages in each *Grosslage* alphabetically and the vineyards alphabetically under each village. Here I have followed him.

I hope that the trouble I have been put to, and the trouble I have taken to explain the trouble I have been put to, will persuade the German authorities to devise some more manageable means of looking up a vineyard name.

*

In common with all other British writers about wine I owe an incalculable debt to the British wine trade. It would be impossible to list here all those of its members who have opened not only their bottles for me in the past, but also their stores of knowledge.

I must mention especially, though, two old friends each of whom took me with him, years ago, on a conducted tour – Fritz Hallgarten in the Rhine regions and the late and much-lamented Otto Loeb in the Mosel.

Then I have been included more than once in visits to Koblenz organized by the hospitable house of Deinhard, and to Worms by the no less hospitable house of Langenbach.

Three generations of the London branch of the former firm have on various occasions been my hosts and my mentors – Charles Hasslacher, at whose ninetieth birthday I assisted, Freddie and Austin, his sons, and his grandson Peter: good friends all.

So, too, father and son of the Hallgarten family – Fritz, already mentioned, and his son Peter: I have drawn much, not only upon luncheon-table discourse with them both, but on the father's books and the son's pamphlets.

Just as I helped to celebrate Charles Hasslacher's ninetieth birthday so, too, I was present at Alfred Langenbach's eightieth: my visits to his cellars and vineyards at Worms were under the auspices of what was then the London firm of

Percy Fox, when among that firm's directors were Denis Stephens-Clarkson, John Surtees, Colin Matheson and Laurence Webber, old friends, good companions and helpful guides. Through them, on one of their most recent visits to Germany, I met Dr Karl Wolfgang Evers of Bonn, a particularly patient guide through the intricacies of the German wine law.

Others to whom I owe many a good bottle and much enlightenment are the late G. W. Thoman, an outstandingly lucid lecturer on German wines, and R. M. Scott of Hellmers Ltd, a shipper with highly idiosyncratic tastes, which it is always a pleasure to hear him expound and explain.

Outside the trade, it was my privilege twenty years ago to sit at the feet of the late Sir Thomas Barlow, in my earliest years as a member of the Athenaeum, where his long chairmanship of the wine committee gave the club's cellar a distinction that its kitchen, alas, has never sought to match.

If he taught me nothing more, I learned from him what dedication the wines of the Mosel can inspire, and I learned much the same about the great sweet hocks from what Otto Loeb told me about John Christie, who, in the early days of Glyndebourne, insisted that only German wines should be served there, and only the sweetest ones, at that.

It was through Otto Loeb, too, that I was privileged to meet the legendary family of Prüm, at Wehlen on the Mosel, and I learned much about the Rheingau and its wines while staying for some days at Schloss Vollrads. I am grateful for their hospitality and their counsel to the late Count Matuschka-Greiffenclau (Richard), to his widow, and to his son Erwin, the present administrator of that noble estate.

I have, indeed, been especially fortunate in my guides to the Rheingau. On my most recent visit, during the 1975 vintage, I was entertained at Schloss Eltz by Count Eltz, an enthusiast, and a highly articulate one, for the wines of his region; and at Schloss Johannisberg, having been briefed in London by Prince Metternich, I was given scholarly guidance by Josef Staab, his *Domänerat*.

A highly personable, and also immensely knowledgeable, guide to this – possibly the greatest – German wine-growing region was Frau Bussmann who, as Ulrike Seyffardt, was the 1972 German Wine Queen. (It must be made clear that each year's German Wine Queen is far from being a sort of Mecca ballroom/Miss World dolly bird. She must be not only of a wine-growing family but herself a wine-grower – the daughter of a wine-grower who had taken up law or physiotherapy would not qualify – she must pass a sort of Master of Wine examination, and she must be presentable and articulate.)

Frau Bussmann is of the family of Diefenhart-Seyffardt, which has been growing wine at Martinsthal for three centuries, and exercises the ancient privilege of opening a *Strasswirtschaft* for three months in every year to sell its own – and only its own – wine by the glass to passers-by.

Another Wine Queen to whom I am indebted is Doris Emmerich, who in 1975 prettily represented her country and another of its delectable products in Moscow, Miami and London, to say nothing of showing Cyril Ray and Reginald Peck around the Nahe.

This was during my most recent visit, already referred to, to the German vineyards, in the course of which I covered 2,250 miles in visiting every one of the country's eleven officially recognized wine-growing regions,[3] from the Ahr valley almost to the Swiss frontier, and from Würzburg in the east to the Saar and Ruwer rivers in the west, filling the gaps in my experience and tying up its all too many loose ends.[4]

3. See page 40.
4. Let it not be supposed that there is any political or ideological significance in there being no mention in this book of any wines from East Germany. A very little is grown in the valley of the Saale, in

The trip was made possible by the generosity of the Stabilisierungsfonds für Wein at Mainz, which in turn was stimulated by the enthusiasm of Geoffrey Godbert and Christine Campbell, of the Wines from Germany Information Service in London, who were unfailingly sympathetic and constructively helpful. Germany's wine industry is lucky in being so ably represented abroad.

Thanks to them and the Stabilisierungsfonds, I was able to take with me my old friend, Reginald Peck, whom I have known for even longer than the nearly thirty years he spent as a British correspondent in Bonn, and whose knowledge of German, the Germans and Germany[5] smoothed our way through many a difficulty, and helped me to understand many a polysyllabic explanation, while his good fellowship and infectious enthusiasm made the whole thing great fun.

In addition to others already mentioned, we were helped and entertained by: Baroness van Zuylen of the house of Deinhard, Koblenz; Riquet Hess of H. Sichel Söhne, Mainz; Else Liedtke and Adolf Steinmann of the Fürstlich Castell'sches Domänenamt, Castell; Dr Reinhold Baumann of the Schlosskellerei, Affaltrach; Hermann Guntrum, Nierstein; Walter

---

Thüringen, but no claim for it is made either by the growers or by the government of the GDR. It is not mentioned in any of the pre-war books on German wines; it is all drunk locally; and on the only two occasions I visited East Berlin, to be stood Soviet caviar at the Adlon, there were wines from Hungary and the Soviet Union on the list, but none from the German Democratic Republic.

These Saale vineyards, south of Jena, lie farther north, I think, even than those of the Ahr valley (q.v.) and, if I am right, are the northernmost on the continent of Europe. Loeb and Prittie, in their *Moselle* (London, Faber, 1972), quote the Swiss reformer, Melanchthon (1497–1560) as saying of Thuringian wines that they were 'sour enough to make the hills weep'. Some of those Swiss reformers must have been good judges of sourness . . .

5. He is the author of *The West Germans: How They Live and Work*, Newton Abbot, David and Charles, 1969.

Schnur, of the house of Buerklin-Wolf, Wachenheim; Karl-Heinz Neiss, of the Deutsches Weintor Cooperative, Ilbesheim; Werner Tyrell, Eitelsbach; Robert Noll of the cooperative Zentralkellerei, Bernkastel; Dr Bernhard Weissensee, the official convenor and assessor of the Lower Franconia tasting panel, Würzburg; and Alban Schueckert, who works eighteen hours a day at the Bavaria state-owned Hofkellerei in the same city, for the sheer pride and joy he takes in the place and its splendid product – the best wine of the region – the living refutation of my capitalist friends' belief that no civil servant can be an enthusiast, no state-owned body competitive, no state product of high quality. Philippe de Rothschild at Mouton is no keener, his wine no better of its kind than Franconia's best.

Much of this book was finally put together in that spacious haven of hush, Brenner's Park-Hotel, Baden-Baden. I am indebted to my old friend Audrey Hooper of Hotel Representatives Inc. for introducing me to so admirable a hostelry in so delightful a town, and to Richard Schmitz, its general manager, for his urbane hospitality.

Finally, my thanks, as always, to my wife, Liz, for her sympathy and patience: she is a keen amateur of the wines of the Mosel and I hope my book does not put her off. Her friend and mine, our secretary, Jennifer Higgie, has typed from my crabbed and cranky manuscript with her customary skill and accuracy.

C.R.

Hawkhurst, Kent
Brenner's Park-Hotel, Baden-Baden, 1975

CHAPTER I

The Wines of Germany

The tribal chieftains of the upper Rhine were drinking wine
long before the Romans came: Greek containers and cups
'made for the complex ceremonials of drinking at the banquets
of aristocrats, or for the simple use of less opulent wine
lovers' found markets there some time during the sixth, fifth
and fourth centuries B C.[1]

What wine, though, did they drink?

Not, it would seem, their own. For, although the grape-
vine is believed to have grown wild on the Rhine and the
Mosel before the Romans ever reached those parts, and
although some scholars hold that the Riesling and the Silvaner
are descended from this *Vitis silvestris*,[2] nevertheless the
general opinion is that it was the Romans who brought the
wine-vine and the art of wine-making there, some time in the
second century A D, and that the wine that was drunk by the
local inhabitants some centuries earlier must have been
imported, like the vessels from which it was drunk, from
Greece or from Magna Graecia (southern Italy).

*

All we know is that although, as Alfred Langenbach wrote,
'since the Roman legionary was used to wine – indeed,
considered it part of his daily ration – he surely initiated

1. Seltman, Charles, *Wine in the Ancient World*, London, Routledge &
Kegan Paul, 1957.

2. Langenbach, Alfred, *German Wines and Vines*, London, Vista
Books, 1962.

viticulture wherever and as soon as he saw a chance, and must have encouraged the local population to take it up and enjoy its products', nevertheless there is no evidence of vine-planting and wine-making in the Rhine and the Mosel valleys less than a couple of centuries after Caesar carried the line of the Gallic frontier to the Rhine, in 57–55 BC.

The wines that the local chieftains drank before that must have come, like the vessels they drank them out of, from south of the Alps.

Some scholars have maintained that the vine was not planted in what is now Germany until the fourth century, but André Simon put it as early as the first,[3] and the poet Ausonius, a Gallo-Roman from Bordeaux (after whom Château Ausone, in St Emilion, is named) who soldiered against the Alamanni in AD 368–9, wrote a long poem in praise of the Mosel which 'made me behold a picture of my own native land, the smiling and well-tended country of Bordeaux – the roofs of country houses, perched high upon the overhanging river-banks, the hill-sides green with vines . . .'[4]

This, surely, is a picture of a region that has been growing wine for more than merely a few decades, especially as Ausonius refers again and again to the 'verdant hills' and their 'fragrant vines', comparing them with other wine-growing countries of the Empire, not only in Gaul but in Macedonia.

So we can at any rate be sure that wine has been made in Germany for at least sixteen hundred years and perhaps eighteen or even nineteen hundred – a precise enough figure for most wine-lovers.

The question, which came first, the wines of the Mosel or the wines of the Rhine, need not detain us here: what is more

3. Simon, André, and Hallgarten, S. F., *The Great Wines of Germany*, London, McGraw-Hill, 1963.

4. Ausonius, with an English translation by Hugh G. Evelyn White (Loeb Classical Library), London, Heinemann, 1919.

important is why both these regions, not particularly favoured by their climates, should have grown wine in the first place and have gone on doing so for almost a couple of thousand years – and wine of high quality at that.

Easy enough to answer the question: why in the first place?

Where the wild vine grows, so will the wine-vine, even if not very successfully or very reliably; where the Roman soldier marched he raised not only his own thirst but that of the native peoples he moved amongst, and although the Romans prided themselves on their supply system it was often no bad thing to produce some of their rations locally. In any case, the locals would not have access to the Roman commissariat.

(The Emperor Domitian's decree of AD 92, ordering the abandonment of half the Empire's vineyards, to protect those of Italy itself, came before those of Germany were planted and was enforced so slackly that German vineyards were almost certainly in being by the time the Emperor Probus repealed the decree in 280.)

Edward Hyams showed in a brilliant piece of exposition[5] why, although the Rhineland generally (and here we may include the Mosel) is if anything slightly less suitable, in climate and in soil, than the southern coasts of Britain for the growing of wine, its vineyards have survived whereas those that once existed in England did not. (The revival of English wine-growing in our time amounts to little more than hobby-farming, profitable though some individual properties may be, and however acceptable their product.)

First, the Frisians, 'those great merchants of the so-called Dark Ages ... skilled boatmen', succeeded in about the seventh century, where others had failed, in navigating the Rhine and carrying its wines to the north-western ports,

5. Hyams, Edward, *Dionysus, a Social History of the Wine Vine*, London, Thames & Hudson, 1965.

whence they were shipped to England and the countries of the north.

These markets remained faithful to their suppliers, who thus found it worth their while to develop the particular qualities of cool-climate wines. This so enhanced the reputation of German wines as to enable them to command high prices, and to make profitable vineyards that should have been uneconomic.

(England was never in this happy position: wines came in from Bordeaux, for three hundred years an apanage of the English crown, at prices that made it uneconomic for Englishmen to grow grapes where grain or fruit could be grown with more consistent success.)

By the ninth century, Charlemagne was presenting great gifts of land, including vineyards named as such, to the princes of the church in his Holy Roman Empire, and his example was followed by his successors.

I have discussed elsewhere[6] to what extent the Church kept alive through the so-called Dark Ages the art and craft of wine-making. Not so great an extent, perhaps, as that devout Catholic, André Simon, maintained.

More, though, perhaps in Germany than in France: at any rate, it is from about the time of those successive imperial gifts and grants that we find records of consistent and substantial exports of German wines to the cities of the Baltic and the Flemish shores and, especially, to London.

Even Henry II of England who, as lord of Aquitaine, owned more French vineyards than the king of France, allowed the merchants of Cologne to sell their wines on the same terms as those of France, and bought Mosel wines for his own household, as did his Plantagenet successors.

When, in 1453, they lost Bordeaux and its vineyards, and

6. Ray, Cyril, *The Wines of France*, London, Allen Lane, 1976 (Penguin edition forthcoming).

French wines in consequence became dearer, those of Germany prospered even more. The trade flourished throughout the remainder of that century and the following – there is mention of Rhenish wine in the *Paston Letters* of the 1490s and in Shakespeare in the 1590s – and it survived the devastation that the Thirty Years' War (1618–48) brought to the vineyards and the carrying trade well enough for Rhenish wine to have graced both Cromwell's table and then Charles II's.

Until about this time all German wine was known in England as 'Rhenish', whatever part of Germany it came from.[7] But by the end of the seventeenth century a distinction was sometimes being made between 'Moselle' – it seems always to have been given what is now the French spelling – and Rhenish, while that in its turn was coming to be named after one or other of the two river ports from which it was shipped: Hochheim and Bacharach.

(Hochheim is above, Bacharach below, the narrows at Bingen: ships of greater draught coming upstream loaded at Bacharach, smaller ships at Hochheim. My guess is that much Mosel wine was shipped through Bacharach, much nearer to where it grew than Hochheim.)

The *Oxford English Dictionary* has traced 'hock' – from Hochheim, by way of Hochheimer and the anglicized 'hockamore' – as far back as 1625, in the works of the dramatist Fletcher; Shakespeare, who died in 1616, was still writing of 'Rhenish'. It is not for another fifty years or so that 'hock' becomes general.

There is no mention at all in the *OED* of Bacharach or its corrupted forms, Bachrag and Backrag, but all were common enough at this period, though completely forgotten now.

*

7. Simon, André L., *History of the Wine Trade in England*, 3 vols., London, Holland Press, 1964 (reissue).

We think of the English eighteenth century as a period when Tory Jacobites drank to 'the king over the water' in claret, and Whigs to the Glorious Revolution and the Hanoverian succession in port.

But it was a time, too, when the gentry at any rate also drank hock, 'either as an aperitif or as a bewildered beverage'.[8]

By 'bewildered', William Younger meant 'mixed', for in Boswell's journals we find 'old hock', so styled, being drunk neat, but Rhenish – presumably younger wine – with sugar, as a sort of cup: 'Friday 8 July [1763] . . . At night I met at the Queen's Head in Holborn with Chandler my printer and Flexney my bookseller. We had a bit of supper, and every man drank his bottle of Rhenish with sugar.'

Not only as a pipe-opener and as a cup, either, but as a straightforward table wine, too, for we know from his cellar books that Walpole preferred Rhenish to French white wines, and shipped the 1706 'Hoghmer' in 1715 – the earliest known reference in English to a vintage hock.[9]

In 1732, the Duke of Chandos was discussing with a Dutch wine-shipper the possibility of buying hocks of the years 1666, 1684 and 1696 – old hocks, indeed![10]

Within four years of its foundation in 1766, the firm of Christie's was listing German wines for sale – 'old hock' in January 1770 at Count de Seilern's house in St James's Square and 'Rennish', in August of the same year, at the Star and Garter public house, bankrupt.[11]

I find a significance that seems to have escaped the scholarly compiler of Christie's sales memoranda in the fact that the

8. Younger, William, *Gods, Men and Wine*, London, Michael Joseph, 1966.

9. Plumb, J. H., *Men and Places*, London, Barrie & Jenkins, 1963.

10. Hodgart, Matthew, 'Doctor Johnson's Wine', in *The Compleat Imbiber, No. 4*, London, Vista Books, 1961.

11. 'Christie's Sale Memorandum 1975–6', No. 5, 13 November 1975 sale.

retiring noble ambassador's German wine was 'old hock' whereas the pub's was 'Rennish', simply.

For a later memorandum quotes Michael Broadbent's article in *Christie's Wine Review* for 1975, which stated that from the early eighteenth to the mid nineteenth century 'heavy, long-matured-in-cask, old hocks were what was expected of a fine German wine',[12] finding supporting evidence in the statement by the editor of the *Journal of the Wine Label Circle* 'that though silver labels of the 18th and early 19th centuries inscribed "Old Hock" abound, "Hock" alone has never been found'.

This latter assertion is not correct.

Penzer lists 'Hock', 'Dinner Hock', 'Premier Hock' and 'Still Hock' as well as 'Old Hock' in his classic work[13] and illustrates an eighteenth-century mother-of-pearl 'Hock' label; a matching 'Rhenish' and 'Old Hock' in the same eighteenth-century escutcheon shape; and a porcelain 'Hock' label.

There was at least one eighteenth-century 'Rhenish' – a Bilston enamel – in the great Hollebone sale of wine labels at Sotheby's in 1955, and the Victoria and Albert Museum's booklet *Bottle-Tickets*[14] illustrates one simple 'Hock' in silver by Phipps and Robinson of 1785 and another by Sandylands Drinkwater of 1770.

And in the very issue of the *Christie's Wine Review* I refer to, a photograph of a 'Hock' label attributed to a Dublin silversmith of 1790 illustrates an article on wine labels by Bernard M. Watney.

The conclusion seems to me inescapable that throughout

12. 'Christie's Sale Memorandum 1975–6', No. 8, 4 December 1975 sale.

13. Penzer, N. M., *The Book of the Wine-Label*, London, Home & Van Thal, 1947.

14. HMSO, London, 1958.

this period hock or Rhenish was one thing, 'old hock' another: the one a poor man's drink (as at the Star and Garter) or for people not so poor on informal occasions (as when Boswell hobnobbed with his printer and his bookseller over 'a bit of supper'), the other for richer folk, such as Sir Robert Walpole and the Duke of Chandos, or for more swagger parties.

The matching pair of escutcheon labels in Penzer, one for 'Rhenish', one for 'Old Hock', is hardly a clincher, for they *may* not have been in the same ownership, but they look as if they were, and powerfully suggest not only that the wines were regarded as basically different, but that both would be drunk by people of the same considerable social standing – such as could afford decanters and silver bottle-tickets – but presumably on different kinds of occasion.

Christie's certainly sold a good deal of old hock throughout the eighteenth century;[15] Captain Gronow, recalling in his debt-ridden old age (*Reminiscences*, 1862) how London's 'best society' lived in Regency times, remembered that 'the wines were chiefly port, sherry, and hock; claret, and even burgundy, being then designated "poor, thin, washy stuff"' – this must indicate old hock; and as late as 1879 Meredith's Dr Middleton, in *The Egoist*, spoke of 'senior Hocks. Their flavours are as a brook of many voices; they have depth also.'

But the *fin de siècle* hock-and-seltzer of Oscar Wilde and his contemporaries must have been mixed with the lightest and youngest wine, such as the good Dr Druitt, in what is still one of the best books in English on wine,[16] was already recom-

15. And on 4 December 1975, for a staggering £250, a half-bottle of the 1727 Rüdesheimer Apostelwein that had been presented at the opening of a great London exhibition of German wines to Mr Roy Hattersley, Minister of State at the Foreign and Commonwealth office, and sold by him for charity.

16. Druitt, Robert, *Report on the Cheap Wines from France, Italy, Austria, Greece and Hungary*, London, Renshaw, 1865.

mending in 1865 to his patients suffering from 'dropsy from liver disease', at £1 a dozen from Fearons.

The book, in spite of its title, does contain some pages on German wines, mentioning 'a thin, sub-fragrant, sub-acid Moselle (Zeltinger)', and 'uncommonly good hock at 16s [a dozen] from Gilbey's of Oxford Street', and observing that 'the higher class of Rhenish (all of which are called *Oc* by our man-servants) differ remarkably in their flavours, but as a rule are all very useful in cases in which we want to support the nervous system, clean the tongue, quench thirst and oxidate the blood'.

So, although Dr Middleton was still to smack his lips over senior hocks, German wines were also being drunk as we drink them now by the earliest years of Victoria's reign: Cyrus Redding, writing in the eighteen-forties,[17] quotes 'a recent author ... with respect to Moselle, and the same will hold good with other wines of Rhenish character' that it had become 'within the last seven years ... a fashionable beverage at the first tables in London'.

The following figures are rough, because they include all wines shipped as 'Rhenish', some of which were bogus compounded sherries from Hamburg, but the proportions are significant: from 1831 to 1862 the consumption of German wines in Britain rose from 58,000 gallons, less than one per cent of the total, to more than 300,000 gallons, nearly 3¼ per cent of the total.[18]

It seems clear from Redding's tribute in the eighteen-forties, Druitt's in the eighteen-sixties, and Shaw's figures, that by this time German wines were much the same in style as those we drink today – light and delicate, flowery as to fragrance

17. Redding, Cyrus, *A History and Description of Modern Wines*, 3rd ed., with additions, London, Bohn, 1851.

18. Shaw, T. G., *Wine, the Vine and the Cellar*, London, Longman Green, 1863.

and, even when late-gathered and sweet, with an underlying acidity that prevented their cloying.

However differently the 'old hocks' were being drunk in the eighteenth and earlier centuries, I have always supposed that the English taste for hock (and wines even approximately of the same style – hence the enormous success since the last war, at the cheaper end of the scale, of Yugoslav rieslings) dates from early Victorian times. For there is reason to believe that an improvement in quality, and thus, no doubt, an increased elegance of style, took place in the first three decades of the nineteenth century.

In 1801, the treaty of Lunéville, between Napoleon and the Emperor of Austria, signing as Holy Roman Emperor, secularized the religious orders of Germany: even André Simon, great believer in the part played by the Church in keeping viticulture alive during the Dark Ages, admitted[19] that the large number of smallholders among whom many of the Church's vineyards were split up now 'took far greater care to make better wine than their fathers, who had farmed the same vineyards for some noble lord, some archbishop or abbot'.

It was some time, of course, before these improved methods of viticulture took effect, but a new era for German wines had dawned. Then, in 1830 the Rhineland authorities decreed an official land register, to include the names of all individual vineyards, with their owners: those that grew the best wine became the best known. And in 1834 the series of customs unions between the various states of Germany, begun on a small scale in 1819, became a *Zollverein* for the whole of Germany: down went the customs barriers between kingdoms and principalities and grand duchies, and up went quality yet again, for in all parts of Germany there was now an increased

19. Simon, André, and Hallgarten, S. F., *The Great Wines of Germany*, London, McGraw-Hill, 1963.

demand for the better wines from the recently named individual vineyards.

All growers who could improve quality by planting the classic vines – notably the Riesling – did so, much to their advantage not only on the home market but also in Britain, for in 1860 Gladstone's budget, although based on a commercial treaty with France and responsible for cheap 'Gladstone claret', reduced the duty on all table wines of whatever provenance. Good German wine now became widely known in Britain.

*

Britain's taste for it survived the phylloxera plague, which set back German wine-growing after the Franco-Prussian War, and then those two greater wars in which the British hock-drinker was ranged against the German wine-grower.

The vine-louse, *Phylloxera vastatrix*, appeared in Germany in about 1875. It did not do such vast damage as it did to France, where wine-growing looms so much larger in the national economy, and where it is said to have cost more money than the war of 1870.[20]

All the same, it was a major set-back – it was still active in the Rheingau as recently as 1927 – and, as in France and almost all the world's other wine-growing countries, it is now kept in check by grafting the classic German vines on to the louse-resistant American root-stocks.

Then there were the two great wars. Clearly, imports came to an end, but during both wars there were stocks enough in Britain for those who had no patriotic objections to go on drinking German wines. The patriotic objections were understandable enough: I think I shared them myself in the last war, in much, if not quite, the same way as I hold *moral* objections now to drinking South African wines.

20. Ray, Cyril, *The Wines of France*, London, Allen Lane, 1976.

It did not take long after 1945 for the trade to pick up, especially as there were now highly respected and much-liked German-Jewish shippers here, particularly knowledgeable about German wines, with old friends from before the war on the Rhine and the Mosel – and if these refugees from Nazi oppression were ready to do business again with Aryan Germans who had stayed in Hitler's Germany, who were we to say otherwise?

Indeed, much of the present prestige of German wines, as well as their commercial success, is owed to what we have been taught by such refugees from Hitler as Alfred Langenbach, Fritz Hallgarten, G. W. Thoman, Otto Loeb and others, and to the scholarship with which they have compiled their lists.

*

It was after 1860, though, as I have shown, that good German wines became more widely known, and not only widely known, but widely enjoyed (though always within the limits I outlined on pages 12–13).

It was twenty years ago that a friend in a family wine-merchant's business, himself already then an old man, told me that his grandfather used to put a higher mark-up on his hocks than his clarets, because 'hock is a rich man's drink'. That must have been a century ago: it is no more merely a rich man's drink now than many a modest French or Spanish wine – look at the two-litre screw-top bottles of Mosel and of Niersteiner in the supermarkets.

Nowadays, as I have already said, the British appreciation of the German *style* extends to wines from other countries than Germany. I could have mentioned Hungary and Romania and South Africa, Austria and northern Italy, as well as Yugoslavia.

But hocks and Mosels are still the exemplars, and while German wines have opened up markets for the others they

32

have not suffered from the competition. Far from it: between 1970 and 1975 consumption of German wines in Great Britain – which is second to the United States as their biggest market, but only just – went up by 150 per cent.

It is not difficult to understand why. There is a family resemblance between all German wines: they come from a relatively small area; they are virtually all white; there is not a great deal – Germany produces about one tenth as much wine as France, less than one tenth as much as Italy, about half as much as California – and nothing like so wide a difference between the commonest and the finest. To my mind, there is a touch of quality about them all: I have drunk many a dull or disappointing German wine, of course, but I have seldom drunk a bad one.

And they are easy to drink and to understand, which does not mean that they are unsubtle: they are easy to drink and to understand in the way that Mozart is easy to listen to (whereas Wagner is not) and that Dickens is easy to read and to understand (whereas Meredith is not). Yet Mozart and Dickens are classics, just as Wagner and Meredith are classics: the wines of Germany – the hocks, the Mosels and the Steinweins – are classics in the same way.

Not a bad sort of classic to be.

CHAPTER 2

The Law and the Label

One of the first articles I wrote about wine was for the woman's page of *The Times*, twenty years or so ago.

I had been asked to discuss German wines, and the eminent shipper whose advice I sought explained how difficult it was to generalize about German wines by pointing out that there were no fewer than 52,000 of them.

The figure was duly quoted in the headline to the article, and my comment was that you could taste one a week for a thousand years – and what an agreeable way of passing the time . . .

Nobody challenged this figure at the time, not even those relentless pickers-up of journalists' inaccuracies, the writers of letters to the editor. Since then, though, I have been given various other figures for the total number of German wines that existed before the present wine law came into effect, each with a distinctive individual name.

They have ranged from about 20,000 to about 50,000, and the variations may have depended on how many different subdivisions were permitted. But attempts to discover the basis for this figure or for that made confusion worse confounded. In any case, whatever the basis of calculation, and whether there were 52,000 of them or a trifling 20,000, there were too many – too many different names, that is. Consumers were confused – and not only consumers. The German wine trade was itself confused, and so were its agents and shippers overseas.

An important aim, if not the main one, of the various

34

bodies set up after the war completely to rewrite the German wine law of 1930, with its untidy train of supplementary provisions, was to reduce the number of vineyard names.

They were reduced to only a little over 3,000 – not the least achievement of the new German wine law: I still give a round figure, though it is correct to within a dozen or so. At the time of writing, there are still some names in dispute or the subjects of appeal.

This enormous change was brought about by ordaining that the smallest geographical unit to be used as the name, or as part of the name, of a wine – the single vineyard, that is, legally defined, and legally obliged to be registered, as being a hillside, slope, valley or natural stretch of land from which wines all of a similar quality and character are usually produced, under the same geological and climatic conditions – should be not less than five hectares (though it can extend up to forty or more if the conditions are met).

This meant an end to the system – if system it can be called – by which any patch of land, perhaps only the size of a tennis-court, or even a billiards-table, had a name of its own if it was individually owned, or if its owner's family had always called it by a name different from another, contiguous, tennis-court-sized patch, also of their own, producing the same wine.

Now, two single but adjoining vineyards, each less than five hectares in extent, producing the same sort of wine because conditions are the same, must both bear the same name even if under separate ownership.

Thus the famous Bernkasteler Doctor, for instance, once a mere 1·35 hectares in the hands of three owners, is now rather more than three and a half hectares in extent, and even that is a concession to its prestige – it should be at least five.

The question naturally arises: has not this caused hard feelings between some neighbours, when a centuries-old name has had to be forgone? The answer to which is, yes. Not so often, though, as might be supposed. Exceptions have been made for small but particularly isolated single vineyards, for small single vineyards (such as the Doctor) that had acquired special markets under their individual names, and in a few other out-of-the-ordinary cases.

*

The new law was to have come into force on 19 July 1971, but in the last stages of its long gestation the European Economic Community issued its regulations 816/70 and 817/70, harmonizing wine legislation for the then six member states.

The German wine law was hastily amended to take account of the EEC regulations, and came into force, oddly enough, earlier than intended, on 14 July 1971, thus affecting the wording of labels on all wines of the 1971 and later vintages, and of non-vintage wines bottled since that date.

The wine law of any member state of the EEC may not be less stringent than EEC regulations prescribe, but is permitted to be more so.

Thus, of the two groups of wine recognized by the EEC as being produced in the member states, 'table wines' and 'quality wines produced in specific regions', the Germans divide the second group into two, and the law governing the official examination of quality wine is more precise than that of other member states, and requires an official examination number to appear on every bottle.

*

It would be as tedious for the reader as for the writer if I were to set down here the whole new German wine law in all its detail.

To put it as briefly as is consistent with clarity, this is how it affects the label on the bottle, and thus how it concerns the consumer:

EEC regulations distinguish between 'table wine' and 'quality wine'. Roughly speaking, a table wine – in German, *Tafelwein* – corresponds to a French non-*appellation vin de table*, but a *Deutscher Tafelwein* more nearly to the sort that in France is given the widest geographical *appellation*, as it might be *vin de Bourgogne*; Beaujolais; or *appellation Bordeaux*.

In Germany, a *Tafelwein* may be a blend of a German wine with wine from another EEC country, in which case it may not be called *Deutscher Tafelwein*, and the words '*Aus Ländern der E.W.G.*' must appear on the label; wine blended with others from non-EEC countries may not be considered even as *Tafelwein*; and only wine made exclusively from grapes harvested in Germany may be described as *Deutscher Tafelwein*, and then only if it comes from one of the following extensive regions (each named after its river) and not blended with the wine of any of the other regions:

Rhein (both banks, from the Neckar to the Ahr)
Mosel (with Saar and Ruwer)
Main (Franconia)
Neckar (Württemberg)
Oberrhein (Baden)

Because of the EEC's zoning of wine-growing areas, the Oberrhein is divided into two zones, but this is of no practical importance to the consumer, and need not concern us here.

As well as one of these five names, the label on a bottle of *Deutscher Tafelwein* may add the name of a sub-region or of a village wine-growing area (as it might be a French *commune*) but not the name of a quality wine-producing region (see below) or of a single vineyard.

It may include the year of the vintage and it must have a minimum of 8·5 per cent alcohol.

No *Tafelwein* or *Deutscher Tafelwein* may bear a *Prädikat* – one of the six distinctions reserved for the finer of the two subdivisions of German 'quality wines produced in specified regions': *Kabinett, Spätlese, Auslese, Beerenauslese, Trocken-beerenauslese* and *Eiswein* (see below).

In practice, *Deutscher Tafelwein* is not exported as such: no British wine-drinker goes into his wine-merchant or his off-licence to ask for a bottle of Oberrhein or of Neckar as he would for a bottle of Beaujolais or of Chianti. Production, in any case, is small: in 1975 only four of the eleven 'quality' regions (see below) produced any *Tafelwein*, which usually accounts for something between 4 and 8 per cent of the total German crop.

More and more, though, such *Deutscher Tafelwein* as is produced and exported will reach overseas markets under brand names, such as 'Goldener Oktober', 'Prinz Rupprecht', or generic fancy names such as 'Moselblümchen' along with a brand name (but not, be it noted, as 'Liebfraumilch' which, with or without a brand name, must be a quality wine – *Qualitätswein*; see page 129).

For all German wines there are regulations similar to (though not always precisely the same as) those of other wine-growing countries governing methods of planting and pruning; types of grape permitted, types temporarily tolerated, and types rigorously forbidden; sites admitted as suitable for viticulture; cellar treatment, and so on.

For the finished *Tafelwein* there is no official tasting test, though the ordinary pure-food and fair-trading laws apply, and in Germany these are strict indeed.

For the two German subdivisions of what EEC regulations regard as one grade, however – '*Qualitätswein bestimmter Anbaugebiete*' (QbA) or quality wine with a site-name, and '*Qualitätswein mit Prädikat*' (QmP) or quality wine with a specific distinction – there are eleven clearly defined and demarcated regions and a most elaborate system of testing, tasting and grading.

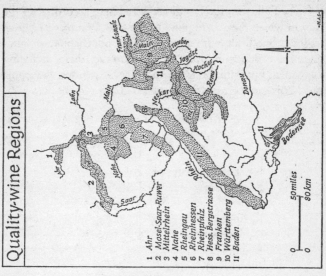

Quality-wine Regions

1 Ahr
2 Mosel-Saar-Ruwer
3 Mittelrhein
4 Nahe
5 Rheingau
6 Rheinhessen
7 Rheinpfalz
8 Hess. Bergstrasse
9 Franken
10 Württemberg
11 Baden

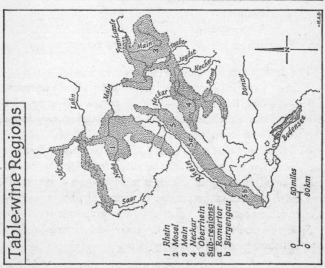

Table-wine Regions

1 Rhein
2 Mosel
3 Main
4 Neckar
5 Oberrhein
Sub-regions:
a Romertor
b Burgengau

First of all, the eleven regions, listed here according to the way in which they correspond to the five *Deutscher Tafelwein* regions, but dealt with later, chapter by chapter, in geographical order, from north to south up the Rhine, including the Mosel, but with the Main and Neckar regions, Franconia and Württemberg, treated as further-flung regions:

| *Quality Wines* | *Tafel Wines* |
11 regions	5 regions
Ahr	
Hessische Bergstrasse	
Mittelrhein	
Nahe	Rhein
Rheingau	
Rheinhessen	
Rheinpfalz	
Mosel–Saar–Ruwer	Mosel
Franken	Main
Württemberg	Neckar
Baden	Oberrhein

The distinctions for QmP wines are:

Kabinett – originally a rather loosely applied term purporting to indicate the grower's own choice of the wines of a particular year – the one he might be supposed to keep in his private *Kabinett* or cupboard.

Now indicates that it has scored at least two points more at the official tasting than the total required for a QbA wine and that, like all other QmP wines, it has not been chaptalized[1] and has the minimum percentage of natural alcohol required – which varies according to district and to grape variety.

Spätlese – made only from late-picked and, therefore, fully ripe bunches, gathered bunch by bunch.

1. See p. 45.

Auslese – may be picked earlier than a *Spätlese*, but all sick or unripe grapes must have been eliminated individually before pressing.

Beerenauslese – picked grape by grape, and only after they have been attacked by *Edelfäule*, or 'noble rot', the *pourriture noble* of the Sauternais, or *Botrytis cinerea*. This usually happens only in mild, moist sunny autumns, and concentrates the sugar in the fruit.[2]

Trockenbeerenauslese – as above, but one stage further, after the grapes have not only rotted but dried on the vine to a withered, sultana-like state, giving even greater concentration of natural sugar.

Eiswein – a peculiarity of cold, northern wine-growing countries: very occasionally found in Alsace, but nowhere else other than Germany. T. G. Shaw[3] refers in 1863 to late vintages in the Rheingau, 'so that frost has frequently set in; the grapes become frozen, and the skins of a reddish-yellow colour. It is believed that this does not deteriorate the quality of the wine, and that the saccharine matter and the alcohol cannot be injured by the cold.'

What happens is that when ripening is so late that the grapes are frozen on the vine, if the berries are picked at below — 8° Centigrade, the water content in the berries is frozen. The grapes are pressed immediately, and the residual juice, separated from the ice, is intensely concentrated in flavour, fragrance and sweetness.

The condition is infrequent;[4] there is hard work involved

2. See p. 45.

3. *Wine, the Vine and the Cellar*, London, Longman Green, 1863.

4. But *Eiswein* itself is becoming less so, and not for the best of reasons. Because of the shortage of pickers, more grapes have to be left for late picking than in the past: some come to be frozen on the vine that would not in the ordinary way make fine wine. Also, there is something of an *Eiswein* cult (as there is a cult for Beaujolais *de l'année* and for *blanc de blancs* champagne): cults put up prices, and some

and considerable loss of quantity: these wines are expensive.

At the time of writing, the word 'Eiswein' may not be used by itself – only in conjunction with one of the other five distinctions. This, however, is still a matter for debate: there are those growers who consider that simply to be an *Eiswein* makes a wine ineligible for any of the other qualifications save, perhaps, 'Kabinett'.

*

If a Bordelais or a Champenois were to argue that the control of vineyard and cellar practice is less precise and rigorous in Germany than in France (notably in the matters of pruning and of permitted yields per acre) the Rhinelander could well answer that this is more than made up for in the severity with which the finished QbA or QmP wine is examined before it is allowed to be offered to the consumer.

First, once the vintage has begun, the grower must register with the local authorities the wines he proposes to produce and present for examination as quality wines, with or without *Prädikat*, though if a *Prädikat* is to be claimed it must be nominated at this stage.

Once in bottle, the wine has to be submitted to state-appointed analysts: they measure and record the proportions in the finished product of sugar, alcohol and acidity, which proportions must reach, and must not exceed, the limits prescribed by law. They would also reject any wine containing foreign matter that indicated improper cellar-practices.

After the wine has been passed by the analyst, three bottles of it are sealed and certificated. Two have to be kept by the grower for two years, in case queries arise as to the quality, or

---

growers make *Eiswein* for purely commercial reasons. It is well to buy only *Eiswein* of what would in any case be a good year.

the efficiency with which it has been tested; the third passes to a state-appointed tasting commission.

Such commissioners – a hundred or so – meet regularly all over the wine-growing regions of Germany, in some places twice a week, in others pretty well every working day.

They consist usually of one representative each of the Land – the regional state government, as it might be of Bavaria, or of Baden-Württemberg[5] – and local consumer-protection bodies, two representative wine-growers and two representatives of the wine trade, but four members form a quorum and there is a panel of reserves.

Members are paid thirteen marks an hour for attending; they elect their chairman afresh at each meeting, though the same man may be elected more than once in succession; they are convened, and their proceedings conducted, by a permanent government official, based locally, who has no vote.

*

Neither had I, when I took part as an unofficial member of the Lower Franconian panel (one of seven for Franconia) meeting in Würzburg, to sit in judgement for rather more than two hours on forty-two 1973 and 1974 Franconian white wines, all QbA candidates except the last, which had been entered as a potential *Spätlese* – which would make it QmP.

We sat in a modern, laboratory-clean, specially designed tasting-room, with a screen between each two seats just big enough to keep the score-cards secret, in front of each of us a

5. Germany's officially designated wine-growing regions do not coincide with the Federal Republic's constituent Länder. Thus, there is no such Land as Franconia, and the wine-growing region of that name lies in Bavaria. The wine-growing region Rheinpfalz comes within the state of Rheinland-Pfalz, but so do the Ahr, Mittelrhein, Nahe, Rheinhesse and Mosel-Saar-Ruwer: the Land produces more than three quarters of Germany's wine.

wash-basin type of spittoon with tap, a hooded light to which to hold up a glass of wine and, to cleanse our palates, fresh bread and cold mineral water.

The official convenor had a file of particulars of every wine under consideration; his assistant poured them for us from anonymous numbered bottles.

All that the panel is allowed to know is the year, the grape, and the grading applied for – not the grower, the bottler, or the district.

The score-card called for marks out of 2 each (0, 1 or 2) for colour and for clarity; out of 4 for nose; and out of 12 for taste.

Proceedings would be held up when any one member was particularly puzzled or put out by any one wine. He would be about to spit, then think again, keep the wine in his mouth, drum his fingers, roll his eyes, shrug his shoulders, spit at last, then catch the chairman's eye and ask for another glass and another opinion.

At the end an average is struck. Eleven out of a possible 20 justifies a wine's being ranked as a quality wine simply (QbA); for QmP wines the qualifying marks are:

QmP	*Kabinett*	13
QmP	*Spätlese*	14
QmP	*Auslese*	15
QmP	*Beerenauslese*	16
QmP	*Trockenbeerenauslese*	17

At our tasting, all the judges were of the opinion that No. 20 had been bottled too warm; No. 27 held up the proceedings, because although it was generally agreed that the vineyard it came from must be too near a pine wood, and that needles must have blown on to it more than was usual, the difference between one member's total award of 9 marks and another's of 13 was too great to permit an acceptable average. The wine was put back to be reconsidered by another panel.

In such a case it is not revealed to the next reviewing panel that a wine has been considered before, and put back for reconsideration: it is simply included in the list as though for the first time.

Thus it was only when we had all turned down No. 42 as a possible *Spätlese*, and passed it only as a *Kabinett*, that the convenor told us that that was exactly what had happened to it six months before, and that the grower had appealed, as was his right.

Of the rest, three were turned down, which meant that they could be sold only as *Tafelwein*, not QbA – one of them was too flabby in taste; one must have been bottled from a dirty cask; one was 'untypical, and not clean'. A grower has the right to be told these decisions, though he is not vouchsafed the detailed markings.

As has already been explained[6] QmP wines may not have their alcoholic strength increased by the addition of sugar before fermentation. This practice, known in France as *chaptalisation*, after the nineteenth-century Dr Chaptal who proposed it, and in Germany as *Gallization* or *Verbesserung*, is resorted to, notably in cool-climate wine-growing areas, when the fully ripe grape still contains insufficient sugar of its own to ferment into the amount of alcohol needed to make proper wine.

Natural sugar, within certain limits prescribed by the law of those countries where it is permitted, is added to the must *before* fermentation so that it, too, ferments into alcohol, bringing it to the required level. Thus, it does not sweeten the wine: the sugar becomes alcohol, and the wine stronger, not sweeter.

In the past, in Germany, wines untreated in this way were

6. p. 40.

designated as *natur* or *naturrein*, but under current German pure-food legislation these terms are now applicable only to foodstuffs containing no preservatives or other additives.

To be sure of obtaining what used to be called a *natur* wine, one buys a QmP wine.

Not to be confused with this *strengthening* by the addition of sugar is the actual *sweetening* of German wine.

Wine can be made – or kept – sweet by checking its fermentation with the addition of brandy, or neutral alcohol, as is done, for instance, to produce port. This is, of course, and always has been, forbidden in Germany: not that any German wine-producer needs forbidding – it is not his job to make a fortified wine.

Fermentation, though, can also be checked by filtering out, before they have completed their work, the yeasts that cause fermentation. This practice is less general than it was, because of its uncertainty. So, too, checking of fermentation by the addition of sulphur dioxide – a method notoriously difficult to control – and by packing ice round the fermenting vats, also something of a hit-and-miss affair.

The method permitted and controlled by law, and followed throughout Germany, is the addition to the fully fermented must of only partially fermented and, therefore, still sweet must, which has been stored in pressure tanks. The law limits the proportion, and requires the juice to be of the same harvesting – same grape, same vineyard site or area, same degree of ripeness, same year – as the must to which it is added.

This particular method is permitted – and is almost universally practised, though in varying degrees, and less in South Germany than elsewhere – to all grades of wine, up to and including *Auslese*. (*Beerenauslese* and *Trockenbeerenauslese* are naturally sweet, and need no such help.)

The reasons for sweetening as distinct from strengthening

are more or less peculiar to German wines and to the German people.

As I have mentioned, in Chapter 1, the German who drinks wine at all (and outside the wine-growing regions themselves most Germans are beer-drinkers rather than wine-drinkers) drinks it after or between meals.

He likes it, therefore, rather sweeter than the Frenchman, the Italian, or the knowledgeable wine-drinking Englishman, who finds that drier wines go better with cooked dishes. For that matter, the North German likes his wine sweeter than does the southerner.

Another explanation I have been given for the need to sweeten German wines, if only slightly, is that because, being cool-climate wines, they are low in alcohol, they would lose their characteristic fragrance and floweriness if they were fermented right out. The natural grape-sugar completely lost in full fermentation would take with it the character of the wine.

(This is what some Germans have told me. My Alsatian friends – and many wine-producers in Franconia – would not agree. They ferment very similar wines much more completely, with certainly no loss of fragrance or flavour. There are no hard and fast rules in matters such as this.)

The advantage of the method I have described, now virtually Germany's only way, and the general practice, is that it is more natural than the use of sulphur dioxide and more controllable than other methods. So much so, indeed, that the same wine can be made much sweeter or only slightly more sweet, according to whether it is intended for sale at home (sweeter) or abroad, in the United States, for instance (not so much so).

A certain amount of German wine, though, is kept dry, by full fermentation and no addition of must. Wine with no more than four grammes of residual sugar per litre may be described on the label as *trocken* – dry. (Subject to certain additional conditions, it may also be described as suitable, with a doctor's consent, for diabetics. In Germany, that is, not in the United Kingdom, where the limit is lower.)

*

As a result of the 1971 wine law, the German wine label has become simpler than it was – and not before time.

I have already mentioned the reduction in the number of vineyard names and the dropping of the words *natur* and *naturrein*. Prizes and distinctions, other than the red German wine seal, the yellow seal for *trocken* wines, and some Baden awards, may no longer be referred to or depicted. Good-bye, alas, to those splendid gold and silver medals from international exhibitions of long ago, bearing the bearded heads of forgotten minor dynasties . . .

Qualitative words such as *feine*, *hochfeine* and *feinste* have disappeared.

It is no longer permitted to use special names (usually saints' days) for harvesting dates, usually denoting exceptionally late gathering and, therefore, unusually high quality: St Nikolaus wine (6 December); Sylvester wine (New Year's Eve); and even Three Kings' wine (6 January, Twelfth Night).

'*Originalabfüllung*' and '*Originalabzug*' for wines matured and bottled in the grower's own cellars are now forbidden: the new permitted designation for the usual English 'estate-bottled', where the grower bottles the wine he has himself produced, is *Erzeugerabfüllung*.

If a shipper or merchant bottles the wine, he is permitted to add the grower's name to his own, but only with the grower's consent.

An example of a typical German wine label, with explanations, is on page 51: there are no deviations from this basic pattern. Some readers may like to check the code number, which is made up of five specific units; the key, by courtesy of Dr Peter Hallgarten, is given on the next page.

*

On some German labels a handsome stylized eagle indicates that the wine comes from a state domain, on others the word *Winzerverein* or *Winzergenossenschaft* that it is the product of a growers' cooperative.

Throughout the following pages there is frequent mention of both, for both play large parts in German wine production.

Cooperatives bring the latest methods and machinery within the reach of Germany's many smallholding growers, and we owe the high general level of German wines largely to the fact that over the whole country some 30 per cent is produced by cooperatives. In the south it is much higher: some 50 per cent in Franconia, 80 in Württemberg, 90 in Baden.[7]

The state domains, though nothing like so big nor so widespread, are similarly influential, for they produce some of the finest wines in the world – Steinberger, to name only one – and their profits go into research institutions, viticultural schools and experimental vineyards. They came into being with Napoleon's secularization of the Rhineland monasteries in 1803; the vineyards then came into the hands of the local princelings and then into those of Germany's present *Länder*.

Some religious houses were secularized as soon as the ragged armies of the first French Republic crossed the Rhine and reached Mainz: on 1 August 1792 Christie's sold a 1726 Hochheim 'imported from the Reduced Convents of Germany'.

7. These approximate figures were given to me by Herr Werner Tyrell, head of the German Wine-Growers' Federation.

How to Read the Code Number

Examination area of quality control	Bottler's village code	Bottler's own individual code	Bottler's actual application number	Year of application
1 = Koblenz	382 [Nierstein]	123		'72 '73
2 = Bernkastel	596 [Piesport]			
3 = Trier			010/72	
4 = Alzey, etc.			10th bottling by this bottler in 1972	

Example: 4·382·263 35/72

4 Examined at Alzey	382 Nierstein	263 Seip's number	35 Seip's 35th application in 1972	72

(1971 Niersteiner Rosenberg Sylvaner Spätlese, Erzeugerabfüllung Seip)

How to Read the German Wine Label

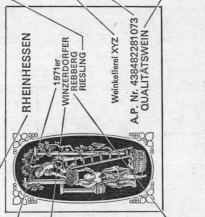

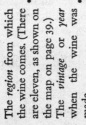

RHEINHESSEN

1971er
WINZERDORFER
REBBERG
RIESLING

Weinkellerei XYZ

A.P. Nr. 43848281073
QUALITÄTSWEIN

(By courtesy of the
Stabilisierungsfonds für Wein, Mainz)

The *variety of grape* used to make the wine; here, a Riesling, Germany's premier grape. Other white varieties include Silvaner, Müller-Thurgau, and Ruländer.

The *name* of the producer or shipper.

Official quality testing number, given by the government to wines passing rigid examination. Found only on *Qualitätswein* and *Qualitätswein mit Prädikat*.

Refers to *category* of wine in bottle. Here, a *Qualitätswein*.

The *region* from which the wine comes. (There are eleven, as shown on the map on page 39.)
The *vintage* or *year* when the wine was made.

The *village* from which the wine comes. Here, the hypothetical village is *Winzerdorf*. And it becomes the name of the wine by adding an 'er' at the end (just as a man from New York is a New Yorker and from London, a Londoner).

The *vineyard* Rebberg surrounding Winzerdorf where grapes were grown from which the wine was made.

CHAPTER 3

The Grapes

One of the valuable leaflets published by the House of Hall-garten lists no fewer than fifteen main varieties of white grapes grown in Germany, five main red varieties, and thirty-seven new crossings (six of them red) that the law permits to be grown.

Of the main white varieties, though, only three account for more than 4 per cent each of the whole – between them, indeed, they account for 80 per cent, with 30·4 per cent of Müller-Thurgau, 26·2 per cent of Riesling and 23·3 per cent of Silvaner, and the next with only 4 per cent.

And only four red varieties account each for more than 4 per cent of the whole – between them, well over 90 per cent.

We need concern ourselves here, then, only with three whites and four reds, as none of the others is likely to be met to any great extent outside Germany or, indeed, outside its own area.

The Riesling is far and away the most widely grown white variety in those regions that produce more of the finest German wines than any other – the Rheingau and the Mosel-Saar-Ruwer – as well as in the Mittelrhein, but it is not quite the most widely grown throughout Germany.

In 1972, the Riesling accounted for 26·2 per cent of all German production, second only to the Müller-Thurgau (30·4 per cent).

The Riesling was recorded as a German wine-producing grape in the fifteenth century: no doubt it was being grown long before that. By the end of the eighteenth century it was certainly the most important variety in the country, and by the middle of the nineteenth probably the most widely grown. It has lost a little ground since then, but more than maintained its reputation.

'The undisputed aristocrat among German vines and grapes',[1] the Riesling is a small yellowish-greenish grape that ripens – later than most – to a yellowish-bronze.

The late ripening is no disadvantage because, contrary to what the late André Simon and Dr Fritz Hallgarten[2] have stated (surprisingly for such authorities), and in spite of its thin skin, it is remarkably resistant to frost, and can be gathered late, fully ripe for *Spätlese* wines; attacked by the *Edelfäule* to be made into the great, sweet *Beerenauslese*, or later still, shrivelled on the vine, for the even greater, sweeter *Trockenbeerenauslese* (see pages 40–41).

Virtually all such wines from the Rheingau and the Mosel-Saar-Ruwer are Rieslings. So, too, are the finest wines of Alsace, across the river.

Even at its most ordinary, wine from the Riesling grape has a balance of fruity sweetness and of fruity acidity that makes it as pleasing in the mouth, and for the same reason, as a ripe strawberry. It is satisfyingly flavoury and yet crisply refreshing.

As Pamela Vandyke Price has put it in her most recent and immensely stimulating book,[3] Riesling wines 'can possess a most elegant fruitiness, and this makes them particularly easy to enjoy at any time of day'.

What is sometimes known as 'the true' Riesling (to distinguish it from the Welschriesling, grown in some parts of Italy and in Central Europe) is known in northern Italy as the Riesling *renano*, or Rhine Riesling, and in California as the

1. Loeb, O. W., and Prittie, Terence, *Moselle*, London, Faber, 1972.
2. *The Great Wines of Germany*, London, McGraw-Hill, 1963.
3. Price, Pamela Vandyke, *The Taste of Wine*, London, Macdonald & Janes, 1975.

Johannisberg Riesling, after the great Schloss Johannisberg of the Rheingau (see page 104). In both regions it grows charming, well-balanced wines, but none of them so fine as those of Germany and Alsace, where a cooler climate and poorer soil give greater delicacy.

So, too, in other parts of northern Italy, in Yugoslavia, Hungary and elsewhere, the Welschriesling – referred to in these regions as a Riesling, simply – shows the family's well-bred characteristics, if in not quite so elegant a form.

*

The Silvaner – in Alsace and elsewhere spelt Sylvaner – is grown almost as widely in Germany as the Riesling. It ripens earlier and will grow in richer soils than the Riesling (which thrives in slate and suchlike arid and unfertile soils), producing larger amounts of, as a rule, softer and blander wine.

It is a noble grape, though, in every sense, and makes the finest wines of Franconia.

*

In recent years the Müller-Thurgau has become Germany's most widely planted vine. It is a cross between the Riesling and the Silvaner,[4] named after the Hermann Müller who invented it at the great Geisenheim viticultural research station in the eighteen-nineties. (Müller was a Swiss: the Thurgau in the name of his grape is the Swiss canton he came from.)

Müller's idea was to combine the grace and charm of the

4. A cross within the same species, not a hybrid, since, strictly speaking, a hybrid is the result of crossing two different species.

In naming a cross, the 'mother' variety, or stock, is placed first, the father second. Thus, the Müller-Thurgau is a Riesling × Silvaner; there is a Silvaner × Riesling called Scheurebe, after Herr Scheu, who brought it about. (*Rebe* is 'grape'.)

Riesling with the bigger yield and earlier ripening of the Silvaner. The measure of his success is not only the acreage under the Müller-Thurgau, but the quality of the wine it produces – it has a touch of the muscatel in taste and an appealingly spicy bouquet.

It is quick to mature in bottle, which is a commercial advantage, and is rather low in acidity. Its success is so recent that it was dismissed pretty perfunctorily in books on German wine written more than a very few years ago: now, however, many authorities maintain that sooner rather than later it will become the archetypal German grape, as the Riesling still is, though already less widely planted.

These experts hold that the quality will improve as the vine acclimatizes itself to soil and to climate.

*

In any consideration of German wines, the reds are of small importance (see Chapter 5) and the four leading varieties of vine that produce them need not detain us long.

Far and away the most widely planted is the Portugieser which accounts for more than 40 per cent of Germany's red-wine production, compared with the 25 of the Spätburgunder. Yet it is not even mentioned in Simon and Hallgarten's great work,[5] published in 1963.

What has turned the tables so quickly is the fact that the Portugieser is prolific and ripens well in unfavourable conditions, whether of soil or climate.

Generally speaking (though much depends on where each variety is grown) the Portugieser gives a lighter wine than the Spätburgunder, with what Alfred Langenbach described[6] as 'a not very refined aroma' – it does not smell very nice.

5. *The Great Wines of Germany*, London, McGraw-Hill, 1963.
6. Langenbach, Alfred, *German Wines and Vines*, London, Vista Books, 1962.

Quite the best of Germany's red wines, such as they are, come from the Spätburgunder, the same grape as the great Pinot Noir, the classic grape of Burgundy, brought thence to Germany, the story goes, by St Bernard of Clairvaux in the twelfth century.

It does not produce in the Rhineland anything like so great a wine as the classic burgundies of the Côte d'Or, but at Assmannshausen, on the Ahr, and in Baden,[7] its best examples have a softness and fruit that the Portugiesers lack.

So, too, do the wines made, in much smaller quantities, from the Trollinger, originally from the Tyrol, which in Württemberg makes a light, fresh wine, not unlike a Loire red, and the Schwarzriesling, which many regard as next to the Spätburgunder in quality and character, but which is not so widely to be found.

7. See Chapters 9, 6 and 14 respectively.

CHAPTER 4

Ripeness Is All

In Germany which, taken as a whole, is the world's most northerly wine-growing country, ripeness is all.

Complete ripeness is not always reached, but as character and capability of maturing depend on sugar-content and its concomitant, alcoholic strength, and as sugar-content derives from the degree of ripeness, it is important that these factors should be known, and to be known they must be measured.

Fortunately, they are measurable.

Hence the frequency with which, in everything said or written about German wine, we come across the word *Oechsle*, which is the measure.

Ferdinand Oechsle (1774–1852) was a chemist of Pforzheim, a Black Forest town between Stuttgart and Karlsruhe. In about 1840 he devised a sort of hydrometer based upon the fact that must – unfermented grape-juice – is heavier than water by the weight of its sugar-content. In his must-scale, therefore, the specific gravity of the must is measured against that of water: the difference is stated as degrees Oechsle, in the figures following the decimal point, omitting the first zero after the point.

Thus a must with a specific gravity of 1·080 is credited with 80 degrees Oechsle, a pretty high German average. A specific gravity of 1·130 gives 130 degrees Oechsle, a figure for a very good *Auslese* or a *Beerenauslese*, and a very fine wine might reach 200 degrees – a specific gravity of 1·200 – or more.

Too much importance can be – and sometimes is – attached to Oechsle degrees. They are measures of sugar-content and, only approximately, of the consequent alcoholic strength, which can sometimes be greater than the Oechsle figures indicate. Especially, though, it must be remembered that a measure of sugar-content, though useful, is not a yardstick for taste in the mouth or fragrance in the nose.

CHAPTER 5

Red, Pink and Sparkling Wines

I am quoted in Fritz Hallgarten's *Rhineland Wineland*[1] as having once written, in an article I had long forgotten: 'German red wines are nothing to write home about so I shall not write home about them . . .'

That must have been a dozen years ago or more, and I have found no reason since to change my opinion: I have drunk some pleasant German red wines in their native country, and enjoyed them, but I can easily understand why they have never been highly prized even at home, much less abroad.

It is not merely that, as Hugh Johnson has observed,[2] 'red wines tend to come from hotter places than white', and that Germany as a whole is a country of cool-climate wines.

White wine needs a measure of acidity to balance its fruit and make it refreshing: an acidity that is lost under a hot, ripening sun. This is true, at any rate to some extent, even of the very sweetest white dessert wines. The reason why many of us prefer the great German *Trockenbeerenauslesen* as dessert wines to even the noblest Sauternes, such as Yquem itself, is that an underlying acidity to the immensely luscious sweetness prevents them from cloying.

In red wines, though, it is tannin that gives both balance – an asperity to balance fruitiness – and staying power, and tannin comes from the skins, pips and stalks of grapes, all

1. Hallgarten, S. F., *Rhineland Wineland*, revised edition, London, Arlington Books, 1965.
2. Johnson, Hugh, *Wine*, London, Mitchell Beazley, revised edition, 1974.

pressed together to make red wine, and needs sunshine for its full development.

Whilst it is true that even the southernmost wine-growing regions of Germany, Baden and Württemberg, lie north of Burgundy – the world's northernmost major red-wine growing region – there are areas there with quite enough sunshine to produce sound red wine.

But tradition, expert knowledge and reputation overseas are factors sometimes as influential as climate and soil.

Germany has been producing and exporting white wines for centuries; Germans know how to grow the sort of grapes that white wines are made from, and how to make such wines; customers overseas want white wines from Germany, not reds.

It is history, as much as geography, that decided the people of the Charentes, between the Loire and Bordeaux, who could grow good table wine if they wanted, to grow a thin sharp wine instead, to distil into cognac.[3] So, too, history as well as geography has made Germany the overwhelmingly white-wine country that it is. There are parts of the country, no farther north than Chinon and Bourgueil on the Loire, where Frenchmen grow red wine, which could produce German red wines of similar quality. Few do.

Such German red wines as are grown do, indeed, remind one to some extent of the reds of the Loire. None has anything like the depth and warmth of a great or even a good burgundy, none is so full of fruit as a Beaujolais, though many are at their most pleasing if drunk in the same way – young and cellar-cool.

One quality, or supposed quality, of German red wine remains to be mentioned.

George Saintsbury, that most overrated of all writers about wine, knew little and cared less about hock and Mosel, the

3. Ray, Cyril, *Cognac*, London, Peter Davies, 1973.

finest of which he found 'palling', preferring the cheapest because 'in these lower qualities, the overpowering and almost barbaric volume of flavour does not occur' and, having enjoyed sparkling Mosel best at the Mitre Hotel, Oxford, with sardine sandwiches, eventually took against it because it 'had a horrible suspicion of the laboratory'.

But he commended what he called 'red hock' and, as Lord Beaverbrook's leader-writers would have said, 'for why?' Because they were 'specifics for insomnia after a fashion which seems to be very little known, even among the faculty'. He preferred them, for this purpose, to hot grog or strong beer.

He might have found an hour or so's coal-mining every day equally efficacious, instead of sitting in his book-lined study writing letters to the public prints recommending that coal-miners should be shot if they went on strike.

Soporific or not – and I have found no one, in Germany or here at home, to endorse the dotty professor's recommendation – 'red hock', as he called it, is a wine of modest pretensions, acceptable enough in its native country, especially after a day of tasting fine white wines, but little more than that.

It is significant that Germany has always been one of the biggest importers of red wines from the south – from Burgundy, the south of France, and from Italy – and it is paradoxical that her own most considerable red-wine growing region is her northernmost, the Ahr (see Chapter 6). But significant again that as it becomes even easier and cheaper, because of the EEC, to import French and Italian red wines, the Ahr is growing fewer reds and more whites.

*

Little pink wine is made in Germany – so little that it is not listed specifically in official statistics: it is included in the figures for red wine. What there is is made – and drunk –

largely in the south: Baden has its *Weissherbst* and Württemberg its *Schillerwein*.

The law distinguishes between the two: *Weissherbst* is a pink wine made from one kind of red grape only – the name of which must appear on the label in the same size lettering as the word *Weissherbst* – pressed as a white wine, which means to say that the must is taken promptly away from the skins.

If more than one type of red grape is used, the wine may only be called *Roseewein*.

Schillerwein is allowed only for QbA and QmP pink wines of Württemberg – made by blending the must of red and white grapes, or from red grapes only. Outside Württemberg, a pink wine made by blending is known as a *Rotling*.

None of these pink wines is worth seeking out anywhere but in its native region.

*

It might be expected that the easy availability of champagne would be affecting the production of *Schaumwein* and *Sekt*, Germany's own sparkling wines, in the same way that the easy availability of French reds is causing German red-wine production to decline. But this is not so.

(The difference between *Sekt* and its cheaper and, therefore, more widely sold, younger brother, *Schaumwein*, is that *Sekt* is required to have nine months' ageing before sale, to meet quality requirements.)

French law defining the *méthode champenoise* is so strict, and the method itself so long drawn out and labour intensive,[4] that the wine is inescapably expensive.

Little *Sekt* that I know of, even the finest, is made by the *méthode champenoise* in its strictest sense, though I have heard of producers in Franconia who follow its principles up to and

4. See Ray, Cyril, *The Wines of France*, London, Allen Lane, 1976, Chapter 3.

including the secondary fermentation in bottle, but not in the bottle in which it is finally to be sold, as is the practice in Champagne. They induce the secondary fermentation in two-litre bottles, from which it is decanted into the bottles destined for sale. And there are small producers of high-quality sparkling wine in the Saar who are said to follow the *méthode champenoise* completely, though I have no first-hand knowledge of their precise methods.

Such manufacturers of *Sekt* are, in any case, in a minority. Virtually all the best *Sekt* and all *Schaumwein* is made by the *cuve close* method, which means that its secondary fermentation takes place in a sealed tank, from which it is bottled under pressure.

The German wine law permits *Sekt* to be termed 'German' and to be accorded a *Prädikat* if it consists of 60 per cent German wine, reaches the required number of 'atmospheres' of pressure, has had nine months' bottle-age, and satisfies such other regulations governing QmP wines as can be applicable to sparkling wines.

In practice, though, good *Sekt* is made exclusively from German wine; better *Sekt* exclusively from the Riesling grapes grown in Germany; and the best at any rate partly, and preferably exclusively, from Saar wines, which have the lightness and acidity, and the cool-climate wine's tendency towards a secondary fermentation in the spring after the vintage, characteristic of champagne itself and essential in the making of fine sparkling wine.

Cheaper sparkling hocks are made, as to their required 60 per cent of German wine (see above), largely from the softer, blander wines of the Mittelrhein and the Rhein-Pfalz (see Chapters 8 and 13).

As a general rule, it is worth looking for a sparkling Mosel, as likely to be lighter and fresher and of better quality than a sparkling hock (or Rheinwein), more likely to be entirely or largely from Riesling grapes, and perhaps partly a Saar wine.

Thus, of a wide range of sound sparklers made by Deinhard at their model plants near Koblenz, the Mosel is dearer than the Cabinet; the 'Cuvée Lila', being guaranteed all Riesling, is dearer still; and the dearest of all, the vintage 'Tradition', has a high proportion of Saar wines, all of them Riesling.

And in the United Kingdom O. W. Loeb and Co. and the Wine Society, both dedicated to quality, list only the Schloss Saarfels Saar Riesling as their German sparkling wine – all Riesling and all from the Saar.

Mention must be made, too, of the estates famous for their still wines, such as Schloss Johannisberg and Steinberg, that sell a proportion of their musts to the specialist makers of *Sekt* to be fermented separately and sold as branded sparkling wines under their own distinguished names. Such wines are respectable, but they are expensive, and though I have never met an indifferent one I have never met one so good of its kind as its still namesake is.

The best and lightest *Sekts* have a fresh, fruity Riesling charm. Are they as good as champagne? Let us say, rather, that they are different. They have at any rate the merit of being cheaper.

Cheaper still in Germany (it is not widely exported) is *Perlwein* which, not so fully effervescent, does not carry the same rate of tax as *Sekt*. It is made, usually by pumping in carbonic acid gas, from cheaper wines not worthy to be made into *Sekt*. Good served cold at a summer picnic, but not to be taken seriously. Nor, indeed, is it allowed to give itself airs above its station: the law forbids its being put up in a bottle with a wired-on cork, covered in foil, as though it were *Sekt*.

Finally, a word about the word, *Sekt*. Some hold that it is a corruption of the French word *sec*, which the Germans have long associated with champagne itself, but for once it seems to me that a more picturesque story is nearer to the truth than the more sober explanation.

Simon and Hallgarten give chapter and verse.[5]

In 1815, the actor Ludwig Devrient played Falstaff in a Shakespearean season at the Court Theatre in Berlin. He used to sup after the theatre at Lutter and Wegner's wine bar, with his crony E. T. A. Hoffmann (of the *Tales*), and, on entering each evening, would cry out the order he had been giving on the stage at the Boar's Head: 'Give me a cup of sack, rogue!'

But the waiter knew that Devrient and Hoffmann's tipple was champagne, not sherris-sack: 'sack' came to mean 'champagne' – or, at any rate, sparkling wine. The phrase caught on: 'sack' became '*Sekt*' and *Sekt* came to mean fizz.

5. *The Great Wines of Germany*, London, McGraw-Hill, 1963.

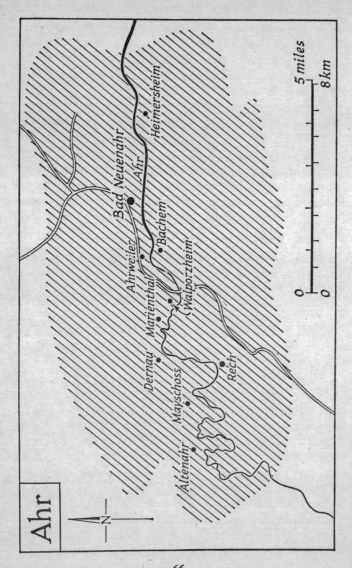

Ahr

N

5 miles
8 km

Heimersheim
Bad Neuenahr
Ahr
Ahrweiler
Bachem
Marienthal
Walporzheim
Dernau
Mayschoss
Rech
Altenahr

CHAPTER 6

The Ahr

Area:	483 hectares
Average crop:	30,000 hectolitres
Types:	57 per cent red
	43 per cent white
Vines:	31 per cent Portugieser
	25 per cent Spätburgunder
	23 per cent Riesling
	16 per cent Müller-Thurgau

The brisk little river Ahr reaches the Rhine halfway between Koblenz and Bonn, within a mile or so of Remagen, where on 7 March 1945 United States troops first crossed the Rhine, after particularly bloody fighting.

To make its Rhine rendezvous, the river has carved through the high, rocky Eifel massif a valley that is outstandingly picturesque even in this region of picturesque river valleys. It twists and turns between thickly wooded bluffs and bare crags, throwing up hill-top castles that look down upon vineyard villages. For the tight turns of the river mean that every few miles there is some corner that catches the sun and the warmth, not only reflected from the surface of the water but that, too, has been stored in surrounding rocky cliffs.

Here, vines have been planted since the third century AD – grapes for red wine since the end of the seventeenth century, when the Pinot Noir was brought from Burgundy, to become the ancestor of the Spätburgunder ('late Burgundy'), which still accounts for 25 per cent of the valley's vines.[1]

For a couple of centuries after its introduction, the Pinot Noir was used not for red wine but for a pink known as *Ahrbleichert* – 'bleached wine' – made by taking the must very quickly off the skins.

Now, although the Ahr still produces more red than white, the white is gaining ground. There has been some degeneration in these parts of the Spätburgunder stock (note how low the average crop is, compared with those of other regions) and, in any case, this is not by nature red-wine country (see page 60).

Except for the northernmost tip of the Mittelrhein (where only white wine is grown, and not very remarkable white wine at that) and the mediocre pockets in eastern Germany, this is the northernmost wine-growing region in the world. It is without challenge as the northernmost red-wine region.

It was all very well for the region to produce red wine when communications were bad, or non-existent, but with cheap red wines easily available from Italy and France – better red wines than those of the Ahr come from Assmannshausen in the Rheingau, and from Baden – there is a continually slackening demand for Ahr reds, reflected in the gradual shift in the annual proportions of reds and whites.

*

Not that Ahr reds will disappear altogether – not, at any rate, for many a year to come. Tradition dies hard in wine-growing, and a family used to tending one kind of vine and making one kind of wine does not turn easily to other kinds.

Skill and experience count, too. It is not only that the Ahrlanders have been making red wine in unfavourable conditions for centuries: they have become good at it. They

1. See Chapter 3.

make better red wine than others would in their valley, or even than other more suitable valleys would produce that have always grown white wine.

Then, too, there is the demand from visitors for what has long been regarded as the typical wine of the region. Not foreign visitors, but German: the Ahr valley is a great place for days out – for evenings out, indeed, from Bonn or Remagen or Koblenz – for week-enders, for walkers, and for summer holidays.

Partly it is the scenery; partly the siren call of the casino at Bad Neuenahr, the nearest legitimate gambling-place for the rich industrialists of the Ruhr (privately owned, but the State takes 80 per cent of the profits); partly the good restaurants in the pretty villages strung along the riverside.

What the rich industrialists expect in pretty riverside restaurants in the Ahr – what the walkers and the week-enders expect in the Ahr valley's little wine-cellars and bars, come to that – is red wine. And, unlike this country, where a walker in the fells or over the moors has long learned not to expect good beer in a country pub, what the German customer expects he is still reasonably likely to get. So the Ahr will go on producing red wine.

The visitor is not likely to come to much harm, however much he drinks – Ahr reds are light in body and low in alcohol. Even if he does, he can always take the cure. Bad Neuenahr is so called, of course, because it is a spa, and millions of British spirit-drinkers must have drunk billions of gallons of its sparkling local mineral water without ever having heard of the Ahr valley: it is called Apollinaris, after the saint whose head, they say, was floated down the Rhine as a present to the Archbishop of Cologne, and it was long the custom of the English man-about-town to ask the barman for his brandy or his whisky with 'a baby Polly' – a small 'split' of Apollinaris.

THE VINEYARDS OF THE AHR

WALPORZHEIM/AHRTAL (*Bereich*)

KLOSTERBERG: *Grosslage*

Weinbauort (village)	*Einzellage (vineyard)*
Ahrweiler	Daubhaus
	Forstberg
	Riegelfeld
	Rosenthal
	Silberberg
	Ursulinengarten
Altenahr	Eck
	Übigberg
Bachem	Karlskopf
	Sonnenschein
	Steinkaul
Bad Neuenahr	Kirchtürmchen
	Schieferley
	Sonnenberg
Dernau	Burggarten
	Goldkaul
	Hardtberg
	Pfarrwingert
	Schieferlay
Heimersheim	Burggarten
	Kapellenberg
	Landskrone
Heppingen	Berg
Marienthal	Jesuitengarten
	Klostergarten
	Rosenberg
	Stiftsberg
	Trotzenberg
Mayschoss	Burgberg
	Laacherberg
	Lochmühlerley

Weinbauort (village)	Einzellage (vineyard)
Mayschoss	Mönchberg
	Schieferley
	Silberberg
Rech	Blume
	Hardtberg
	Herrenberg
Walporzheim	Alte Lay
	Domlay
	Gärkammer
	Himmelchen
	Kräuterberg
	Pfaffenberg

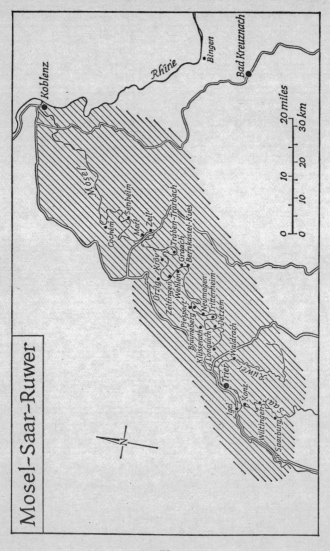

CHAPTER 7

Mosel–Saar–Ruwer

Koblenz

Rhine

Bingen

Bad Kreuznach

Mosel

Cochem
Senheim
Mert
Zelt
Traben-Trarbach
Kröv
Graach
Bernkastel-Kues
Ürzig
Zeltingen
Wehlen
Neumagen
Trittenheim
Piesport
Dhron
Braunberg
Detzem
Klüsserath
Longuich
Waldrach
Igel
Trier
Konz
Ruwer
Wiltingen
Saar
Saarburg

20 miles

30 km

20

10

10

20

10

0

0

Mosel-Saar-Ruwer

Area:	10,714 hectares
Average crop:	900,000 hectolitres
Type:	All white
Vines:	74 per cent Riesling
	13 per cent Müller-Thurgau
	11 per cent Elbling

This region and the much smaller Rheingau together make up less than one fifth of Germany's wine-growing area, but they produce more of its finest, or, at any rate, its most highly prized and most highly priced, wines than the other nine regions put together.

On the whole, Mosel wines at their most characteristic are lighter and more delicate than the fuller, deeper Rheingaus – sopranos compared with contraltos, say, or tenors with baritones – but, as with the two great French reds, clarets and burgundies, there is a family resemblance, too, and some overlapping of style.

It is the soil and the grape that make *Moselwein* – slate and the Riesling.

Just as in Toynbee's theory that civilization is a response to challenge – but to a challenge that *can* be met – so the world's most delicate wines are grown where the vine has to struggle for survival, but where it *can* survive. In the valley of the Mosel and its tributaries, the cool northern climate and the poorness of the soil make a struggle necessary, but the deep valley is sheltered from the keen winds and the sharp frosts that sweep and bite the hilltops, and the slate holds moisture and reflects heat.

Although the Mosel flows generally a little east of north, its winding is such that it often flows due west or due east, so that vineyards on its right bank or its left face south, as do those of the Rheingau. In addition, the recent canalization of the Mosel has not only made transport easier and cheaper but has increased the surface of water above each lock, and with it the reflection of warmth and light on to the vines.

The Upper Mosel, above Trier, is chalky country, and its grapes are not as a rule the Riesling but Müller-Thurgau, Elbling and others. Those wines of moderate quality that grow here are sold locally at modest prices that make them good value. The thinner, sharper wines go to the makers of *Sekt*.

The Lower Mosel, from Zell to Koblenz, does grow the Riesling but its slate is too hard: most of the wines are undistinguished.

The greatest wines of the region come from the Middle Mosel and the valleys of the two small tributaries, the Saar and the Ruwer.

Bernkastel dominates the Middle Mosel, a vulgarly picturesque souvenir-shop town, but enchanting at night when the ruins of Landshut on the hill above the town are floodlit – a castle in the air – and surrounded by the green corduroy of the most valuable vineyards in Germany.

All the famous names are here – Piesport and Brauneberg, Bernkastel and Graach and Wehlen, and Zeltingen. As Hugh Johnson has observed, it is impossible to place them in order:

the least of these wines should be something of very obvious personality; almost water-white with a gleam of green and with 40 or 50 little bubbles in the bottom of the glass, smelling almost aggressively

74

of grapes, filling and seeming to coat your mouth with sharpness, sweetness and scent.[1]

Locally, and very unlike the southern regions, it is the sweetness that is prized. Whereas, as I have recounted in a later chapter, the list of Baden wines at Brenner's Park-Hotel in Baden-Baden begins with a dozen *trocken* wines, there is not a single such in the list of fifty-nine Mosel wines at the Hotel zur Post in Bernkastel – there are only a couple of *herb* wines, which are not so dry, and the proprietor's wife was surprised when we asked her for the driest open wine she had as an aperitif and more than surprised – astonished – when we asked for another glass of the same.

Partly, no doubt, it is a matter of the relative sophistication of one hotel's clientèle and the other's, but it is also a matter of geography. The wines of the south have more body, and can be dry without being sharp. Here, in what is virtually the world's most northerly wine-growing area of any size, when there is not enough sunshine for sweetness, the wines are thin and acid, suitable only for *Sekt*.

The wines of the Saar and the Ruwer are excellent examples. To use Lichine's words,[2] Saar wines 'in the great years are almost super-Mosel in their development of the characteristic elements of *race* and steely elegance' and the Ruwer wines 'at their best, are the lightest of Germany ... In the best years they have a bouquet suggesting cinnamon, but in poorer years they may be too acidic for most tastes.'

For a long time now the generic title Moselblümchen – 'little flowers of the Mosel' – has been permitted to a Mosel wine with up to one third admixture from other regions. It has not been decided, at the time of writing, whether more precise regulations shall be applied to it such as those that

1. *Wine*, revised edition, London, Mitchell Beazley, 1974.
2. *Encyclopaedia of Wines and Spirits*, London, Cassell, 1975.

permit Liebfraumilch to be a QbA wine. So far, it is a *Tafel-wein* only, and never more than a very modest example of the more superficial Mosel characteristics.

THE VINEYARDS OF MOSEL–SAAR–RUWER
BERNKASTEL (*Bereich*)

BADSTUBE: *Grosslage*

Weinbauort (village)	*Einzellage (vineyard)*
Bernkastel-Kues	Bratenhöfchen
	Doctor
	Graben
	Lay
	Matheisbildchen

BEERENLAY: *Grosslage*

Lieser	Niederberg-Helden
	Rosenlay
	Süssenberg

KURFÜRSTLAY: *Grosslage*

Andel	Schlossberg
Bernkastel-Kues	Johannisbrünnchen
	Kardinalsberg
	Rosenberg
	Schlossberg
	Stephanus-Rosengärtchen
	Weissenstein
Brauneberg	Hasenläufer
	Juffer
	Juffer-Sonnenuhr
	Kammer
	Klostergarten
	Mandelgraben

Weinbauort (village)	Einzellage (vineyard)
Burgen	Hasenläufer
	Kirchberg
	Römerberg
Kesten	Herrenberg
	Paulinsberg
	Paulinushof berger
Lieser	Schlossberg
Maring-Noviand	Honigberg
	Kirchberg
	Klosterberg
	Römerpfad
	Sonnenuhr
Mülheim	Amtsgarten
	Elisenberg
	Helenenkloster
	Sonnenlay
Osann-Monzel	Kätzchen
	Kirchlay
	Paulinslay
	Rosenberg
Veldenz	Carlsberg
	Elisenberg
	Grafschafter Sonnenberg
	Kirchberg
	Mühlberg
Wintrich	Grosser Herrgott
	Ohligsberg
	Sonnenseite
	Stefanslay

MICHELSBERG: *Grosslage*

Hetzerath	Brauneberg
Minheim	Burglay
	Günterslay
	Kapellchen
	Rosenberg

Weinbauort (village)	*Einzellage (vineyard)*
Neumagen-Dhron	Engelgrube
	Grafenberg
	Grosser Hengelberg
	Hofberger
	Laudamusberg
	Rosengärtchen
	Roterd
	Sonnenuhr
Piesport	Domherr
	Falkenberg
	Gärtchen
	Goldtröpfchen
	Günterslay
	Schubertslay
	Treppchen
Rivenich	Brauneberg
	Geisberg
	Niederberg
	Rosenberg
Sehlem	Rotlay
Trittenheim	Altärchen
	Apotheke
	Felsenkopf
	Leiterchen

MÜNZLAY: *Grosslage*

Graach	Abtsberg
	Domprobst
	Himmelreich
	Josephshöfer
Wehlen	Klosterberg
	Nonnenberg
	Sonnenuhr
Zeltingen-Rachtig	Deutschherrenberg
	Himmelreich

Weinbauort (village)	*Einzellage (vineyard)*
Zeltingen-Rachtig	Schlossberg
	Sonnenuhr

NACKTARSCH: *Grosslage*

Kröv	Burglay
	Herrenberg
	Kirchlay
	Letterlay
	Paradies
	Steffensberg

PROBSTBERG: *Grosslage*

Fell	Maximiner Burgberg
Kenn	Held
	Maximiner Hofgarten
Longuich	Hirschlay
	Maximiner Herrenberg
Mehring	vineyards on the right
	side of the Mosel
Riol	Römerberg
Schweich	Annaberg
	Burgmauer
	Herrenberg

SANKT MICHAEL: *Grosslage*

Bekond	Brauneberg
	Schlossberg
Detzem	Maximiner Klosterlay
	Würzgarten
Ensch	Mühlenberg
	St Martin
	Sonnenlay
Klüsserath	Bruderschaft
	Königsberg
Köwerich	Held
	Laurentiuslay

Weinbauort (village)	Einzellage (vineyard)
Leiwen	Klostergarten
	Laurentiuslay
Longen	Goldkupp
	Zellerberg
Lörsch	Goldkupp
	Zellerberg
Mehring	Blattenberg
	Goldkupp
	Zellerberg
Pölich	Held
	Südlay
Schleich	Klosterberg
	Sonnenberg
Thörnich	Enggass
	Ritsch

SCHWARZLAY: *Grosslage*

Bausendorf	Herzlay
	Hubertuslay
Bengel	sites not chosen
Burg	Falklay
	Hahnenschrittchen
	Schlossberg
	Thomasberg
	Wendelstück
Dreis	Johannisberg
Enkirch	Batterieberg
	Edelberg
	Ellergrub
	Herrenberg
	Monteneubel
	Steffensberg
	Weinkammer
	Zeppwingert
Erden	Busslay
	Herrenberg

Weinbauort (village)	Einzellage (vineyard)
Erden	Prälat
	Treppchen
Flussbach	Reichelberg
Hupperath	Klosterweg
Kinheim	Hubertuslay
	Rosenberg
Lösnich	Burgberg
	Försterlay
Platten	Klosterberg
	Rotlay
Traben-Trarbach	Burgweg
	Gaispfad
	Hühnerberg
	Königsberg
	Kräuterhaus
	Kreuzberg
	Schlossberg
	Taubenhaus
	Ungsberg
	Würzgarten
	Zollturm
Traben-Trarbach (Ortsteil Starkenburg)	Rosengarten
Traben-Trarbach (Ortsteil Wolf)	Auf der Heide
	Goldgrube
	Klosterberg
	Schatzgarten
	Sonnenlay
Ürzig	Würzgarten
Wittlich	Bottchen
	Felsentreppche 1
	Klosterweg
	Kupp
	Lay
	Portnersberg
	Rosenberg

81

VOM HEISSEN STEIN: *Grosslage*

Weinbauort (*village*)	Einzellage (*vineyard*)
Briedel	Herzchen
	Nonnengarten
	Schäferlay
	Schelm
	Weisserberg
Pünderich	Goldlay
	Marienburg
	Nonnengarten
	Rosenberg
Reil	Falklay
	Goldlay
	Moullay-Hofberg
	Sorentberg

OBERMOSEL (*Bereich*)

GIPFEL: *Grosslage*

Bitzingen	sites not chosen
Fellerich	Schleidberg
Fisch	sites not chosen
Helfant-Esingen	Kapellenberg
Kirf	sites not chosen
Köllig	Rochusfels
Kreuzweiler	Schloss Thorner Kupp
Meurich	sites not chosen
Nittel	Blümchen
	Hubertusberg
	Leiterchen
	Rochusfels
Oberbillig	Hirtengarten
	Römerberg
Onsdorf	Hubertusberg
Palzem	Karlsfelsen
	Lay

Weinbauort (village)	Einzellage (vineyard)
Portz	sites not chosen
Rehlingen	Kapellenberg
Soest	sites not chosen
Tawern	sites not chosen
Temmels	Münsterstatt
	St Georgshof
Wasserliesch	Albachtaler
	Reinig auf der Burg
Wehr	Rosenberg
Wellen	Altenberg
Wincheringen	Burg Warsberg
	Fuchsloch

KÖNIGSBERG: *Grosslage*

Edingen	sites not chosen
Godendorf	sites not chosen
Grewenich	sites not chosen
Igel	Dullgärten
Langsur	Brüderberg
Liersberg	Pilgerberg
Mesenich	Held
Metzdorf	sites not chosen
Ralingen	sites not chosen
Wintersdorf	sites not chosen

SAAR-RUWER (Bereich)

RÖMERLAY: *Grosslage*

Franzenheim	Johannisberg
Hockweiler	sites not chosen
Kasel	Dominikanerberg
	Herrenberg
	Hitzlay
	Kehrnagel
	Nieschen

Weinbauort (village)	*Einzellage (vineyard)*
Kasel	Paulinsberg
	Timpert
Korlingen	Laykaul
Mertesdorf	Felslay
	Johannisberg
	Mäuerchen
Mertesdorf (Ortsteil Maximin Grünhaus)	Abtsberg
	Bruderberg
	Herrenberg
Morscheid	Dominikanerberg
	Heiligenhäuschen
Riveris	Heiligenhäuschen
	Kuhnchen
Sommerau	Schlossberg
Trier	Altenberg
	Andreasberg
	Augenscheiner
	Benediktinerberg
	Burgberg
	Deutschherrenberg
	Deutschherrenköpfchen
	Domherrenberg
	Hammerstein
	Herrenberg
	Jesuitenwingert
	Karthäuserhofberg Burgberg
	Karthäuserhofberg Kronenberg
	Karthäuserhofberg Orthsberg
	Karthäuserhofberg Sang
	Karthäuserhofberg Stirn
	Kupp
	Kurfürstenhofberg
	Leikaul

Weinbauort (village)	*Einzellage (vineyard)*
Trier	Marienholz
	Maximiner
	Rotlay
	St Martiner Hofberg
	St Matheiser
	St Maximiner Kreuzberg
	St Petrusberg
	Sonnenberg
	Thiergarten Felsköpfchen
	Thiergarten unterm Kreuz
Waldrach	Doktorberg
	Ehrenberg
	Heiligenhäuschen
	Hubertusberg
	Jesuitengarten
	Jungfernberg
	Krone
	Kurfürstenberg
	Laurentiusberg
	Meisenberg
	Sonnenberg

SCHARZBERG: *Grosslage*

Ayl	Herrenberger
	Kupp
	Scheidterberger
Filzen	Altenberg
	Herrenberg
	Liebfrauenberg
	Pulchen
	Steinberger
	Unterberg
	Urbelt
Hamm	Altenberg
Irsch	Hubertusberg
	Sonnenberg

Weinbauort (village)	Einzellage (vineyard)
Irsch	Vogelsang
Kanzem	Altenberg
	Hörecker
	Schlossberg
	Sonnenberg
Kastel-Staadt	König Johann Berg
	Maximin Staadt
Könen	Fels
	Kirchberg
Konz	Auf der Kupp
	Brauneberg
	Euchariusberg
	Falkensteiner Hofberg
	Klosterberg
	Sprung
Mennig	Altenberg
	Euchariusberg
	Herrenberg
	Sonnenberg
Oberemmel	Agritiusberg
	Altenberg
	Hütte
	Karlsberg
	Raul
	Rosenberg
Ockfen	Bockstein
	Geisberg
	Heppenstein
	Herrenberg
	Kupp
	Neuwies
	Zickelgarten
Pellingen	Herrgottsrock
	Jesuitengarten
Saarburg	Antoniusbrunnen
	Bergschlösschen

Weinbauort (village)	*Einzellage (vineyard)*
Saarburg	Fuchs
	Klosterberg
	Kupp
	Laurentiusberg
	Rausch
	Schlossberg
	Stirn
Schoden	Geisberg
	Herrenberg
	Saarfeilser Marienberg
Serrig	Antoniusberg
	Helligenborn
	Herrenberg
	Hoeppslei
	König Johann Berg
	Kupp
	Schloss Saarfelser Schlossberg
	Schloss Saarsteiner
	Vogelsang
	Würtzberg
Wawern	Goldberg
	Herrenberger
	Jesuitenberg
	Ritterpfad
Wiltingen	Braune Kupp
	Braunfels
	Gottesfuss
	Hölle
	Klosterberg
	Kupp
	Rosenberg
	Sandberg
Estate	Scharzhofberger
	Schlagengraben
	Schlossberg

ZELL/MOSEL (*Bereich*)

GOLDBÄUMCHEN: *Grosslage*

Weinbauort (village)	*Einzellage (vineyard)*
Briedern	Rüberberger Domherrenberg
Bruttig-Fankel	Götterlay
Cochem	Bischofstuhl
	Herrenberg
	Hochlay
	Klostergarten
	Pinnerkreuzberg
	Schlossberg
	Sonnenberg
Ellenz-Poltersdorf	Altarberg
	Kurfürst
	Rüberberger Domherrenberg
Ernst	Feuerberg
	Kirchlay
Klotten	Brauneberg
	Burg Coreidelsteiner
	Rosenberg
	Sonnengold
Moselkern	Kirchberg
	Rosenberg
	Übereltzer
Müden	Funkenberg
	Grosslay
	Leckmauer
	St Castorhöhle
	Sonnenring
Pommern	Goldberg
	Rosenberg
	Sonnenuhr
	Zeisel
Senheim	Römerberg
	Rüberberger Domherrenberg
Treis-Karden	Dechantsberg

Weinbauort (village)	*Einzellage (vineyard)*
Treis-Karden	Juffermauer
	Münsterberg

GRAFSCHAFT: *Grosslage*

Alf	Arrasburg-Schlossberg
	Burggraf
	Herrenberg
	Hölle
	Kapellenberg
	Katzenkopf
	Kronenberg
Beuren	Pelzerberger
Bremm	Calmont
	Frauenberg
	Laurentiusberg
	Schlemmertröpfchen
Bullay	Brautrock
	Graf Beyssel-Herrenberg
	Kirchweingarten
	Kroneberg
	Sonneck
Ediger-Eller	Bienenlay
	Calmont
	Elzogberg
	Engelströpfchen
	Feuerberg
	Höll
	Osterlämmchen
	Pfaffenberg
	Pfirsichgarten
	Schützenlay
Neef	Frauenberg
	Petersberg
	Rosenberg
Nehren	Römerberg
St Aldegund	Himmelreich

Weinbauort (village)	*Einzellage (vineyard)*
St Aldegund	Klosterkammer
	Palmberg-Terrassen
Zell-Merl	sites not chosen

ROSENHANG: *Grosslage*

Beilstein	Schlossberg
Bremm	Abtei
	Kloster Stuben
Briedern	Herrenberg
	Kapellenberg
	Römergarten
	Servatiusberg
Bruttig-Fankel	Kapellenberg
	Layenberg
	Martinsborn
	Pfarrgarten
	Rathausberg
	Rosenberg
Cochem	Arzlay
	Nikolausberg
	Rosenberg
Ellenz-Poltersdorf	Silberberg
	Woogberg
Mesenich	Abteiberg
	Deuslay
	Goldgrübchen
Senheim	Bienengarten
	Rosenberg
	Vogteiberg
	Wahrsager
Treis-Karden	Greth
	Kapellenberg
	Treppchen
Valwig	Herrenberg
	Palmberg
	Schwarzenberg

SCHWARZE KATZ: *Grosslage*

Weinbauort (village)	*Einzellage (vineyard)*
Senheim	Rüberberger Domherrenberg
Zell	Burglay-Felsen
	Domherrenberg
	Geisberg
	Kreuzlay
	Nussberg
	Petersborn-Kabertchen
	Pommerell
Zell-Kaimt	Marienburger
	Römerquelle
	Rosenborn
Zell-Merl	Adler
	Fettgarten
	Klosterberg
	Königslay-Terrassen
	Stefansberg
	Sonneck

WEINHEX: *Grosslage*

Alken	Bleidenberg
	Burgberg
	Hunnenstein
Burgen	Bischofstein
Dieblich	Heilgraben
Güls	Bienengarten
	Im Röttgen
	Königsfels
	Marienberg
Hatzenport	Burg Bischofsteiner
	Kirchberg
	Stolzenberg
Kattenes	Fahrberg
	Steinchen
Kobern-Gondorf	Fahrberg

Weinbauort (village)	*Einzellage (vineyard)*
Kobern-Gondorf	Fuchshöhle
	Gäns
	Kehrberg
	Schlossberg
	Uhlen
	Weissenberg
Koblenz, Ortsteil Lay	Hubertsborn
Koblenz, Ortsteil Moselweiss	Hamm
Lehmen	Ausoniusstein
	Klosterberg
	Lay
	Würzlay
Löf	Goldblume
	Sonnenring
Moselsürsch	Fahrberg
Niederfell	Fächern
	Goldlay
	Kahllay
Oberfell	Brauneberg
	Goldlay
	Rosenberg
Winningen	Brückstück
	Domgarten
	Hamm
	Im Röttgen
	Uhlen

Not yet assigned a *Grosslage:*

Senheim	Lay

CHAPTER 8

Mittelrhein

Area:	945 hectares
Average crop:	70,000 hectolitres
Type:	99 per cent white
	1 per cent red
Vines:	83 per cent Riesling
	9 per cent Müller-Thurgau
	4 per cent Silvaner

Officially, this region stretches from a point just downstream[1] from Bingen, where the Nahe joins the Rhine, to the outskirts of Bonn, but little wine is grown, in few vineyards, beyond its midway point, Koblenz.

In fact, the Mittelrhein is the smallest but two of the eleven quality-wine regions of Germany. Only the Ahr and the Hessische Bergstrasse are smaller, whereas the next biggest, the Rheingau, is three times the size of the Mittelrhein.

Nor are its wines remarkable, but the scenery is, for the Rhine is at its most romantic between Bingen and Koblenz,

1. Downstream just enough to leave Assmannshausen in the Rheingau. This may seem odd, for the reds of Assmannshausen are no more characteristically Rheingau wines than Mittelrhein, and the confluence of Nahe and Rhine looks a logical point to mark a boundary. There is a historical reason, though. Assmannshausen falls within the boundaries of the old walled fiefdom of the Rheingau (see p. 105), the northern limit of which was along the river Wisper, which joins the Rhine at Lorch.

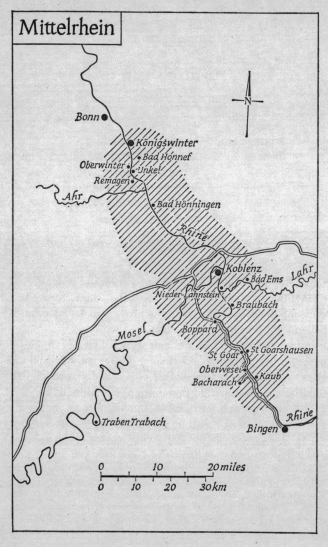

Mittelrhein

N

Bonn

Königswinter
Bad Honnef
Oberwinter
Unkel
Remagen

Ahr

Bad Hönningen

Rhine

Koblenz
Bad Ems
Lahr
Nieder-Lahnstein
Braubach

Mosel

Boppard

St Goar
St Goarshausen
Oberwesel
Bacharach
Kaub

Traben Trabach

Rhine
Bingen

0   10   20 miles
0   10   20   30 km

with its castle-like crags and its craggy castles, its legend of the Lorelei, its mice who ate the bishop, and the reefs and the rapids of the Binger Loch ('Bingen Hole').

(It is appropriate that it was here, at Koblenz, that Karl Baedeker should have set up shop, as a printer and bookseller, and that the first of his great guide books, published in 1839, early in the Romantic tourist boom, should have been a guide to the Rhine.)

It is to the Binger Loch that the Mittelrhein wines owe the fame that once they had. Frank Schoonmaker, after observing of the Mittelrhein that 'this is a viticultural district of which, despite its spectacular beauty, I can say very little and would as soon leave unsaid what I have to say',[2] goes on to recall that Bacharach (see page 96) and its sister-town, Kaub, on the opposite bank, were once as celebrated as Nierstein and Johannisberg, but that this was when there were no railways and few roads, so that the German wine trade depended on the river. Bacharach and Kaub were well to the seaward – or customers' – side of the dangerous passage of the Binger Loch and 'became more famous as centres of the wine trade than distinguished for the wines which their own vineyards produced'.

Today, these wines are little known outside their own region. Indeed, they are almost all drunk locally, and there is not enough there to go round: both better wines and cheap wines come in from other districts.

Here is a striking illustration of how climate – in this case a mere micro-climate – affects wine-growing.

The Mittelrhein is contiguous to the Rheingau, where grow the noblest wines of Germany, and it grows the same sort of grape. But it turns the corner: whereas the Rheingau faces south, and benefits from longer hours of sunshine and the heat and light reflected from the river, as well as being protected

2. Schoonmaker, Frank, *German Wines*, London, Oldbourne, 1957.

by the hills at its back from the cold, the Mittelrhein vineyards, according to which bank they lie on, face east or west, and are plagued by the east winds that whistle down the valleys of the Rhine tributaries from the Taunus.

So it is only in sheltered corners, and, elsewhere, only in very good years, that Mittelrhein wines attain real distinction; when they do, they resemble Mosel wines rather than those of the Rheingau, for the grapes never attain Rheingau ripeness, and the clay-slate soil is very similar to that of the Mosel.

At their best, therefore, they have delicacy and bouquet; at their most typical, they lack body, and are much used for making into Sekt.

The widest area of wine-growing is on the left bank, around Bacharach (the name of which is said to derive from that of Bacchus), a walled town gay with window-boxes and picturesque with half-timbered houses and Gothic churches. Opposite is Kaub, another picture-postcard town, where Blücher crossed the Rhine to march against Napoleon (there is a Blücher museum).

Three things remain to be mentioned about the Mittelrhein.

Its furthest tip, at the edge of Bonn, the Königswinter, really is the northernmost point on the continent at which a widely known wine is grown – farther north than the Ahr, the Mosel, or Champagne. (Bonn is one minute of latitude north of Bournemouth, and has much colder winters.)

I am told that there are vineyards near St Goarshausen that have never suffered the phylloxera, but none of their wines has come my way.

Neither has any of the region's one per cent of red wine, made from the Spätburgunder in the Siebengebirge, or Seven Mountains, near Königswinter, across the river from Bonn.

One of the seven mountains is the Drachenfels, or Dragon Rock, now tramped by trippers – it is said to be the most-climbed hill in the world – but once frequented by a dragon,

the dragon that Siegfried slew, before bathing in its blood.
I need hardly add that the wine is called Dragon's Blood.

THE VINEYARDS OF MITTELRHEIN
BACHARACH (*Bereich*)

SCHLOSS REICHENSTEIN: *Grosslage*

Weinbauort (*village*)	*Einzellage* (*vineyard*)
Niederheimbach	Froher Weingarten
	Reifersley
	Schloss Hohneck
	Soonecker Schlossberg
Oberheimbach	Klosterberg
	Römerberg
	Sonne
	Wahrheit
Trechtingshausen	Morgenbachtaler

SCHLOSS STAHLECK: *Grosslage*

Bacharach	Hahn
	Insel Heylesern Wert
	Kloster Fürstental
	Mathias Weingarten
	Posten
	Wolfshöhle
Bacharach/Steeg	Hambusch
	Lennenborn
	St Jost
	Schloss Stahlberg
Manubach	Heilgarten
	Langgarten
	Mönchwingert
	St Oswald
Oberdiebach	Bischofshub
	Fürstenberg

Weinbauort (village)	*Einzellage (vineyard)*
Oberdiebach	Kräuterberg
	Rheinberg

RHEINBURGENGAU (*Bereich*)

BURG HAMMERSTEIN: *Grosslage*

Bad Hönningen	Schlossberg
Dattenberg	Gertrudenberg
Hammerstein	Hölle
	In den Layfelsen
	Schlossberg
Kasbach	Stehlerberg
Leubsdorf	Weisses Kreuz
Leutesdorf	Forstberg
	Gartenlay
	Rosenberg
Linz	Rheinhöller
Rheinbrohl	Monte Jup
	Römerberg
Unkel	Berg
	Sonnenberg

BURG RHEINFELS: *Grosslage*

St Goar-Werlau	Ameisenberg
	Frohwingert
	Kuhstall
	Rosenberg

GEDEONSECK: *Grosslage*

Boppard	Elfenlay
	Engelstein
	Fässerlay
	Feuerlay
	Mandelstein
	Ohlenberg
	Weingrube

Weinbauort (village)	Einzellage (vineyard)
Brey	Hämmchen
Rhens	König Wenzel
	Sonnenlay
Spay	Engelstein

HERRENBERG : Grosslage

Dörscheid	Kupferflöz
	Wolfsnack
Kaub	Backofen
	Blüchertal
	Burg Gutenfels
	Pfalzgrafenstein
	Rauschelay
	Rosstein

LAHNTAL : Grosslage

Bad Ems	Hasenberg
Dausenau	Hasenberg
Fachbach	sites not chosen
Nassau	Schlossberg
Obernhof	Goetheberg
Weinähr	Giebelhöll

LORELEYFELSEN : Grosslage

Bornich	Rothenack
Kamp-Bornhofen-Kestert	Liebenstein-Sterrenberg
	Pilgerpfad
Nochern	Brünnchen
Patersberg	Teufelstein
St Goarshausen	Burg Katz
	Burg Maus
	Hessern
	Loreley-Edel

MARKSBURG: *Grosslage*

Weinbauort (village)	*Einzellage (vineyard)*
Braubach	Koppelstein
	Marmorberg
	Mühlberg
Filsen	Pfarrgarten
Koblenz-Ehrenbreitstein	Kreuzberg
Lahnstein	Koppelstein
Osterspai	Liebeneck-Sonnenlay
Urbar	Rheinnieder
Vallendar	Rheinnieder

SCHLOSS SCHÖNBURG: *Grosslage*

Damscheid	Frankenhell
	Goldemund
	Sonnenstock
Dellhofen	Römerkrug
	St Wernerberg
Langscheid	Hundert
Niederburg	Bienenberg
	Rheingoldberg
Oberwesel	Bernstein
	Bienenberg
	Goldemund
	Ölsberg
	Römerkrug
	St Martinsberg
	Sieben Jungfrauen
Perscheid	Rosental
Urbar b. St Goar	Beulsberg

Not yet assigned a *Grosslage*:

Hirzenach	Probsteiberg

CHAPTER 9

The Rheingau

Area:	3,035 hectares
Average crop:	210,000 hectolitres
Types:	98 per cent white
	2 per cent red
Vines:	78 per cent Riesling
	11 per cent Müller-Thurgau
	6 per cent Silvaner

Without a map to remind us, we often think of the Rhine as a south-to-north river, but from Mainz, where it is joined by the Main, to Bingen, where it is joined by the Nahe, it flows from east to west.

So, for twenty miles or so of its course, the vineyards of the right bank face the south and the sun. And the right bank of the Rhine here is nearly all vineyards: they rise, more gently than those of other German riverside vineyards – those of the Mosel, for instance, and the Mittelrhein – to the wooded crest of the Taunus mountains.

These hills and woods shield them from northerly and easterly winds, while the broad surface of the river itself throws back on to them the warmth of the sun and then, in autumn, the mists that so bedevil the timetable at Frankfurt airport, but here prolong the summer's warmth and encourage the *Edelfäule* – the 'noble rot' – that makes possible the richest and most lusciously sweet *Beerenauslese* and *Trockenbeeren-auslese* dessert wines of Germany.

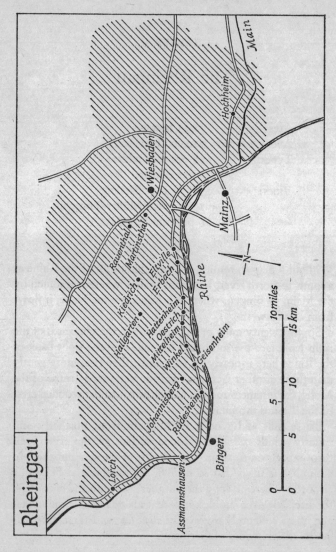

Rheingau

Lorch

Assmannshausen

Bingen

Rüdesheim

Johannisberg

Winkel

Geisenheim

Mittelheim

Oestrich

Hattenheim

Hallgarten

Kiedrich

Erbach

Eltville

Martinsthal

Rauenthal

Wiesbaden

Hochheim

Mainz

Main

Rhine

N

0   5   10   15 km
0   5   10 miles

This is the Rheingau, 'the climax', as Hugh Johnson has put it, 'of the wine-growing Rhine'.[1]

With the exception of that southernmost strip of German soil that borders Lake Constance, this is the region – taking one year with another – with the most sunshine, the mildest climate, and the greatest freedom from frost and snow, of all West Germany.

Generally speaking, the Rheingau's climate is milder, even, than that of the Rheinpfalz, which lies farther to the south, but is less protected by hills, and less fully exposed to the sun, because it is flatter and does not face south to its direct warmth and the reflected warmth from the river.

The soil of the Rheingau is rich, too – much richer than the slate of the Mosel, the chalk of Champagne and the gravel of the Médoc – and what does not bear grapes for wine bears dessert fruit with an almost Italian abundance. I have dined in mid-August at Schloss Vollrads, in the very middle of the Rheingau, and found the last course to be a heaped bowl of peaches and apricots as fine as any I have eaten on any of the shores of the Mediterranean, and the sweetest and ripest of those exquisitely sweet little Mirabelle plums, hardly bigger than cherries – all grown as near to the table at which we were dining as the bottles of Schloss Vollrads that followed each other majestically throughout the meal.

Each bottle contained the archetypal Rheingau wine – full, soft, fruity, yet superbly well balanced. There are German wines with greater delicacy than those of the Rheingau – the best of the Mosel-Saar-Ruwer wines for instance – and there are others, such as those of Franconia, that are more suitable, because of their dryness, to drink with savoury dishes. But there are few or none with more character, more fullness of body 'and above all', in a phrase from Simon and Hallgarten's

1. Johnson, Hugh, *The World Atlas of Wine*, London, Mitchell Beazley, 1971.

great book,[2] 'an aristocratic distinction or "breeding"'. And few white wines have such capacity for ageing. They vie with the best white burgundies to be considered the greatest white wines in the world.

Amongst German wines, too, there are more of the greatest names here than in any comparable area – the Rheingau is a mere thirty kilometres by seven. Schloss Johannisberg and Schloss Vollrads, owned by noblemen, and the wines of Rauenthal and Marcobrunn, some also from noble estates, some from state domains, and of Steinberg, entirely state-owned, have made the Rheingau famous in the same way that Lafite, Latour and Mouton have brought renown to the *commune* of Pauillac.

Here, too, at Geisenheim, is the greatest of Germany's many state-controlled schools of viticulture, now more than a century old; here, too, the state-owned monastery, Kloster Eberbach, built between 1150 and 1200, where the great Steinberger wine is made and cellared, and where the German Wine Academy's courses for members of the wine trade and amateurs of wine attract students from as far afield as Australia and Japan.

Rüdesheim is a sort of riverside Southend or Coney Island, where the rude mechanicals of the Rhine – and from farther afield – come for the day, the week-end or the summer fortnight to drink themselves into the mood for wearing funny hats and buying gewgaws. (For more scholarly visitors there is the Brömserburg Wine Museum, with an English-speaking guide.)

It is oddly out of keeping with the reputation of the Rheingauers themselves who, in a country as conscious of regional differences – of differences between very small regions very near to each other – as is Italy, are considered not only by others but by themselves as a peculiarly stiff-necked people.

2. *The Great Wines of Germany*, London, McGraw-Hill, 1963.

More estates here than elsewhere are under patrician ownership – a *Freiherr* or so, some barons, two or three princes, and
four or five counts, some of whose families have been growing
wine on these same estates for five hundred years or more.
(Count Eltz who came from the other side of the river to a
property long owned, but not lived in, by his family a mere
thirty-five years ago has heard himself described as 'a johnny-
come-lately', to use his own translation of a derogatory
German term.)

It is partly this tradition of aristocratic landowning that
gives Rheingauers in general the reputation of being lordly,
compared say with the lighter-hearted folk of the Mosel, but
partly too the tiny region's history of independence.

Throughout the Middle Ages and into the seventeenth
century, the Rheingau defended itself against outsiders – even
for long periods against its liege lord, the Elector of Mainz –
with a fence of beech trees specially pruned, trained and bent
to form an impenetrable thicket, fifty paces deep, with stone
watch-towers at the corners of the rectangle. There was a
shibboleth by which to detect outsiders – only a native
Rheingauer would call a fine wine *e foi Woiche* – its effects
mitigated by a law of sanctuary and naturalization: if the city
fathers of Winkel allowed a stranger to stay for twenty-four
hours he became a Rheingauer, whatever his accent.

The fortress-wall of living trees was not breached until the
Thirty Years' War, and was still in being more than a century
later. Its long continuance has meant that the boundaries of the
Rheingau have always been clearly defined and are still well
understood – along the river Wisper from Lorch, parallel with
the Rhine, and then at a right angle down to Walluf.

This, no doubt, is why Assmannshausen is officially included
in the Rheingau, although geographically it could as well be
included in the Mittelrhein, and although its red wines are in
no way kin to the Rheingau Rieslings.

The red wine of Assmannshausen is the most highly regarded in Germany – more so than that of the Ahr. Here, too, as there, there has been in the past a decline in the quality of Spät-burgunder, a matter put right by replanting.

The wine is lighter, both in colour and in body, than the red wines of Burgundy, from the same grape. There is a rare but otherwise unjustifiably expensive sweet pink Assmanns-hausen made from late-gathered grapes, the must taken from the skins earlier than for a red wine, and I recently tasted a 1966 pink Assmannshausen *Eiswein* that went charmingly with fruit, both to look at and to drink, but not in the same memorable class as a Riesling would have been.

History has placed Assmannshausen within the Rheingau, and the same is true of Hochheim, for although it is a dozen miles or more beyond the Rheingau's eastern boundary, and not on the Rhine at all, but the Main, it was long in allegiance to the Elector of Mainz as part of his Rheingau fiefdom.[3]

In any case, the Hochheimers have all the Rheingau characteristics, if not to so marked a degree as Schloss Vollrads, say, or Steinberger, but comparable with all but the very best – soft, delicate and well balanced, with a slight earthy taste of their own that is discerned by more discriminating palates than mine.

It has been explained in an earlier chapter how from Hoch-heim derives the English word for all Rhine wines – hock.

Here, perhaps, is the place for a pleasing legend.

It was a grower of the Rheingau who told me one summer's day over a glass of wine on a Rhine hotel terrace how 'your Queen Victoria visited these parts in 1850' (which, indeed, she did: it is in the history books) 'and took particularly to the wines of Hochheim'.

This, too, is true. She gave permission for one vineyard there to be rechristened the Königin Victoriaberg; a tower

3. See footnote on p. 93.

in the vineyard bears witness, and so does the wine's exuberant label, with the royal arms.

My guide and mentor went on: 'and she so loved Germany, and the beautiful wines of Germany, and especially the wines of Hochheim, that every time she sat down to dine she used to raise her glass and cry' (and he suited the actions to the word, raised glass, raised voice and all) 'your good Queen Victoria would lift her glass and cry, "A bottle of hoc' keeps away the doc." '

THE VINEYARDS OF THE RHEINGAU

JOHANNISBERG (*Bereich*)

BURGWEG: *Grosslage*

Weinbauort (*village*)	*Einzellage* (*vineyard*)
Assmannshausen-Aulhausen	Berg Kaisersteinfels
Geisenheim	Fuchsberg
	Mäuerchen
	Mönchspfad
	Rothenberg
Lorch	Bodental-Steinberg
	Kapellenberg
	Krone
	Pfaffenwies
	Schlossberg
Lorchhausen	Rosenberg
	Seligmacher
Rüdesheim	Berg Roseneck
	Berg Rottland
	Berg Schlossberg
	Bischofsberg
	Drachenstein
	Kirchenpfad
	Klosterberg
	Klosterlay

Weinbauort (village)	*Einzellage (vineyard)*
Rüdesheim	Magdalenenkreuz
	Rosengarten

DAUBHAUS: *Grosslage*

Flörsheim	Herrnberg (divisible)
Hochheim	Berg (divisible)
	Domdechaney
	Herrnberg (divisible)
	Hofmeister
	Hölle
	Kirchenstück
	Königin Viktoriaberg
	Reichesthal (divisible)
	Sommerheil
	Stein
	Stielweg
Kostheim	Berg (divisible)
	Reichesthal (divisible
	Steig
	Weiss Erd
Wicker	Goldene Luft
	König Wilhelmsberg
	Nonnberg
	Stein

Not yet assigned a *Grosslage* :

Frankfurt/Main	Lohberger Hang

DEUTELSBERG: *Grosslage*

Erbach	Hohenrain
	Honigberg
	Marcobrunn
	Michelmark
	Schlossberg
	Siegelsberg
	Steinmorgen

Weinbauort (village)	*Einzellage (vineyard)*
Hattenheim	Engelmannsberg
	Hassel
	Heiligenberg
	Mannberg
	Nussbrunnen
	Pfaffenberg
	Schützenhaus
	Wisselbrunnen
Estate	Steinberg

ERNTEBRINGER: *Grosslage*

Geisenheim	Kilzberg
	Klaus
	Kläuserweg
	Schlossgarten
Johannisberg	Goldatzel
	Hansenberg
	Hölle
	Mittelhölle
Estate	Schloss Johannisberg
	Schwartzenstein
	Vogelsang
Mittelheim	Edelmann (divisible)
	Goldberg
	St Nikolaus (divisible)
Winkel	Dachsberg

GOTTESTHAL: *Grosslage*

Östrich	Doosberg
	Klosterberg (divisible)
	Lenchen
Estate	Schloss Reinhartshausen

HEILIGENSTOCK: *Grosslage*

Eltville	Sandgrub (divisible)

Weinbauort (*village*)	*Einzellage* (*vineyard*)
Kiedrich	Gräfenberg
	Klosterberg
	Sandgrub (divisible)
	Wasseros

HONIGBERG: *Grosslage*

Mittelheim	Edelmann (divisible)
	St Nikolaus (divisible)
Estate	Schloss Vollrads
Winkel	Bienengarten
	Gutenberg
	Hasensprung
	Jesuitengarten
	Klaus (divisible)
	Schlossberg

MEHRHÖLZCHEN: *Grosslage*

Hallgarten	Hendelberg
	Jungfer
	Schönhell
	Würzgarten
Östrich	Klosterberg (divisible)

REGION OF MELSUNGEN

Böddiger	Berg

STEIL: *Grosslage*

Assmannshausen	Frankentha
Assmannshausen-Aulhausen	Hinterkirch
	Höllenberg

STEINMÄCHER: *Grosslage*

Dotzheim	Judenkirch
Eltville	Langenstück
	Rheinberg

Weinbauort (village)	Einzellage (vineyard)
Eltville	Sandgrub (divisible)
	Sonnenberg
	Taubenberg
Frauenstein	Herrenberg
	Homberg
	Marschall
Martinsthal	Langenberg
	Rödchen
	Wildsau
Niederwalluf	Berg Bildstock
	Oberberg
	Walkenberg
Oberwalluf	Fitusberg
	Langenstück
Rauenthal	Baiken
	Gehrn
	Langenstück
	Nonnenberg
	Rothenberg
	Wülfen
Schierstein	Dachsberg
	Hölle

CHAPTER 10

The Nahe

Area:	4,206 hectares
Average crop:	240,000 hectolitres
Type:	90 per cent white
	10 per cent red and/or pink
Vines:	32 per cent Silvaner
	30 per cent Müller-Thurgau
	25 per cent Riesling
	13 per cent various crosses

When the Directors' Wine Club[1] was set up, in 1959, and I was invited to construct its first wine-list, my policy was to keep it short, to begin with; to see that each wine was typical of its kind, to help members to get used to identifying different styles of wine; and, of course, to find wines that were cheap or, at any rate, good value for money.

There was room for one German wine and I approached an old friend, Freddie Hasslacher, then head of the House of Deinhard, to find me just such a hock: it had to speak for Germany, as it were; to be immediately likeable as well as easily recognizable; and the best value he could offer.

Freddie needed little time for thought: 'It'll have to be a Nahe wine,' he said, and from its very beginning the Directors' Wine Club listed a Schloss Böckelheimer Riesling produced (I

1. Now merged, along with the Women's Wine Club, into Peter Dominic's Wine Mine Club: I am no longer associated with it.

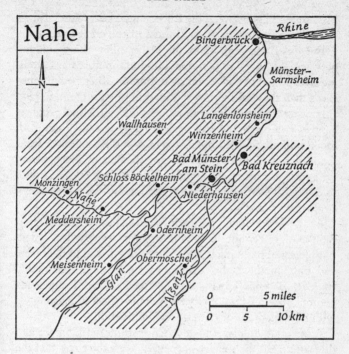

presume, because of its modest price) by one of the many admirable cooperatives of the region. It was non-vintage, of course, and it was re-ordered every six months or so, to make sure the wine was always fresh: it remained a members' favourite for long after the German list was extended.

Schloss Böckelheimer was our choice because Nahe wines seem to sum up German wines (or, rather, the wines of the better-known German regions – I exclude those of the south, Franconia, Württemberg and Baden, as being different in style from those of the Rheingau and the Mosel, Rheinhessen and Rheinpfalz).

Many authorities say that it is because geographically the

Nahe region lies between the Rheingau and the Mosel that its wines are a sort of synthesis of those of the other two.

But this is too glib. True, the Nahe valley as a whole lies between the other two rivers, but the vineyards are along the river's lower reaches, much nearer the Rheinhessen vineyards than those of the Mosel – marching with them, in fact.

If many find the Rheingau richness and the Mosel crispness happily combined and balanced in Nahe wines, others find, too, a reminder of Rheinpfalz spiciness and Rheinhessen fruit. 'Intrinsically German', said Cyrus Redding of Nahe wines, well over a century ago,[2] and a German Wine Queen once told me that someone had called the region 'the tasting-room of German wines'.

As will be seen from the statistics at the head of this chapter, the three great white-wine vines are very evenly distributed, but plenty of space is left for new strains – it was in the Nahe, and only in the Nahe, that I came across the remarkably fragrant Bacchus cross – and in 1962 Alfred Langenbach commented[3] on the activity of Nahe growers in keeping up with new methods of training and cultivation.

A big state domain and research institute set the pace and the pattern for the smaller properties, with the result that the general level of quality is high, and the variety of style unusually wide.

Not only is there a greater range of vines than in most other regions of wine-growing Germany but there is a greater range of soil. There are slate, clay and volcanic rock; the great cliff of Rotenfels, at the bend of the river near Bad Münster, at the foot of which grows one of the finest wines of the region, is clearly and dramatically of red sandstone; the

2. Redding, Cyrus, *A History and Description of Modern Wines*, 3rd ed., with additions, London, Bohn 1851.

3. Langenbach, Alfred, *German Wines and Vines*, London, Vista Books, 1962.

Kupfergrube patently springs from copper-bearing soil; and the stone-polishing and jewellery industries of Idar-Oberstein, at the western end of the vineyard stretches of the Nahe, came into being four hundred years ago because of the local deposits of agate, amethyst and jasper. Stretches at this end of the vineyard area are described as being of porphyry soil.

The villages of the Nahe are not so pretty or so picturesque as those of the Rheingau, say, and not so much visited, but Bad Kreuznach – city, so the locals say, of nightingales and roses – and Bad Münster, both at the very heart of the best vineyards of the region, are charming little spa towns.

Charming is perhaps the word, too, for even the most modest Nahe wines – the very finest, such as those of Kreuznach and Niederhäuser, can claim more important descriptions – and perhaps there is no better way to drink them than in a rose-garden, listening to the nightingales.

THE VINEYARDS OF THE NAHE
KREUZNACH (*Bereich*)

KRONENBERG: *Grosslage*

Weinbauort (village)	*Einzellage (vineyard)*
Bad Kreuznach	Agnesienberg
	Berg
	Breitenweg
	Brückes
	Forst
	Galgenberg
	Gutental
	Himmelgarten
	Hinkelstein
	Hirtenhain
	Hofgarten
	Höllenbrand
	Honigberg

Weinbauort (village)	*Einzellage (vineyard)*
Bad Kreuznach	Hungriger Wolf
	In den Mauern
	In den 17 Morgen
	Junker
	Kahlenberg
	Kapellenpfad
	Katzenhölle
	Krötenpfuhl
	Mollenbrunnen
	Mönchberg
	Monhard
	Narrenkappe
	Nonnengarten
	Osterhöll
	Paradies
	Römerhalde
	Rosenberg
	Rosenheck
	Rosenhügel
	St Martin
	Schloss Kauzenberg
	Steinberg
	Steinweg
	Tilgesbrunnen
	Vogelsang
Bretzenheim	Felsenköpfchen
	Hofgut
	Pastorei
	Schlossgarten
	Vogelsang
Dalberg	Ritterhölle
	Schlossberg
	Sonnenberg
Gutenberg	Felseneck
	Römerberg
	St Ruppertsberg

Weinbauort (village)	Einzellage (vineyard)
Gutenberg	Schlossberg
	Schloss Gutenburg
	Sonnenlauf
Hargesheim	Mollenbrunnen
	Straussberg
Hergenfeld	Herrschaftsgarten
	Mönchberg
	Sonnenberg
Schöneberg	Schäfersley
	Sonnenberg
Sommerloch	Birkenberg
	Ratsgrund
	Sonnenberg
	Steinrossel
Spabrücken	Höll
Wallhausen	Backöfchen
	Felseneck
	Hasensprung
	Höllenpfad
	Hörnchen
	Johannisberg
	Kirschheck
	Laurentiusberg
	Mühlenberg
	Pastorenberg
	Sonnenweg

SCHLOSSKAPELLE: *Grosslage*

Bingen-Bingerbrück	Abtei Ruppertsberg
	Hildegardisbrünnchen
	Klostergarten
	Römerberg
Burg Layen	Hölle
	Johannisberg
	Rothenberg
	Schlossberg

Weinbauort (village)	Einzellage (vineyard)
Dorsheim	Burgberg
	Goldloch
	Honigberg
	Jungbrunnen
	Klosterpfad
	Laurenziweg
	Nixenberg
	Pittermännchen
	Trollberg
Eckenroth	Felsenberg
	Hölle
Genheim	Rossel
Guldental	Apostelberg
	Hipperich
	Hölle
	Honigberg
	Rosenteich
	St Martin
	Sonnenberg
	Teufelsküche
Laubenheim	Fuchsen
	Hörnchen
	Junker
	Karthäuser
	Krone
	St Remigiusberg
	Vogelsang
Münster-Sarmsheim	Dautenpflänzer
	Kapellenberg
	Königsschloss
	Liebehöll
	Pittersberg
	Rheinberg
	Römerberg
	Steinkopf
	Trollberg

Weinbauort (village)	*Einzellage (vineyard)*
Rümmelsheim	Hölle
	Johannisberg
	Rothenberg
	Schlossberg
	Steinköpfchen
Schweppenhausen	Schlossgarten
	Steyerberg
Waldlaubersheim	Alteburg
	Bingerweg
	Domberg
	Hörnchen
	Lieseberg
	Otterberg
Weiler	Abtei Ruppertsberg
	Klostergarten
	Römerberg
Windesheim	Breiselberg
	Fels
	Hausgiebel
	Hölle
	Römerberg
	Rosenberg
	Saukopf
	Schäfchen
	Sonnenmorgen

SONNENBORN: *Grosslage*

Langenlonsheim	Bergborn
	Königsschild
	Lauerweg
	Löhrer Berg
	Rothenberg
	St Antoniusweg
	Steinchen

SCHLOSS BÖCKELHEIM (*Bereich*)

BURGWEG: *Grosslage*

Weinbauort (village)	Einzellage (vineyard)
Altenbamberg	Kehrenberg
	Laurentiusberg
	Rotenberg
	Schlossberg
	Treuenfels
Bad Münster a. St-Ebernburg	Erzgrupe
	Felseneck
	Feuerberg
	Götzenfels
	Höll
	Köhler-Köpfchen
	Königsgarten
	Luisengarten
	Rotenfelser im Winkel
	Schlossberg
	Steigerdell
	Stephansberg
Duchroth	Felsenberg
	Feuerberg
	Kaiserberg
	Königsfels
	Rothenberg
	Vogelschlag
Niederhausen an der Nahe	Felsensteyer
	Herrmannsberg
	Hermannshöhle
	Kertz
	Klamm
	Pfaffenstein
	Pflingstweide
	Rosenberg
	Rosenheck
	Steinberg

Weinbauort (village)	Einzellage (vineyard)
Niederhausen an der Nahe	Steinwingert
	Stollenberg
Norheim	Dellchen
	Götzenfels
	Kafels
	Kirschheck
	Klosterberg
	Oberberg
	Onkelchen
	Sonnenberg
Oberhausen an der Nahe	Felsenberg
	Kieselberg
	Leistenberg
	Rotenberg
Schlossböckelheim	Felsenberg
	Heimberg
	In den Felsen
	Königsfels
	Kupfergrube
	Mühlberg
Traisen	Bastei
	Kickelskopf
	Nonnengarten
	Rotenfels
Waldböckelheim	Drachenbrunnen
	Hamm
	Kirchberg
	Kronenfels
	Marienpforter Klosterberg
	Muckerhölle
	Mühlberg
	Römerberg

PARADIESGARTEN: *Grosslage*

Alsenz	Elkersberg
	Falkenberg

Weinbauort (village)	Einzellage (vineyard)
Alsenz	Hölle
	Pfaffenpfad
Auen	Kaulenberg
	Römerstich
Bayerfeld-Steckweiler	Adelsberg
	Aspenberg
	Mittelberg
	Schloss Stolzenberg
Boos	Herrenberg
	Kastell
Desloch	Hengstberg
	Vor der Hölle
Feilbingert	Bocksberg
	Feuerberg
	Höchstes Kreuz
	Kahlenberg
	Königsgarten
Gaugrehweiler	Graukatz
Hochstätten	Liebesbrunnen
Kalkofen	Graukatz
Kirschroth	Lump
	Wildgrafenberg
Lauschied	Edelberg
Lettweiler	Inkelhöll
	Rheingasse
Mannweiler-Coelln	Rosenberg
	Schloss Randeck
	Seidenberg
	Weissenstein
Martinstein	Schlossberg
Meddersheim	Altenberg
	Edelberg
	Liebfrauenberg
	Präsent
	Rheingrafenberg
Meisenheim	Obere Heimbach

Weinbauort (village)	Einzellage (vineyard)
Merxheim	Hunolsteiner
	Römerberg
	Vogelsang
Monzingen	Frühlingsplätzchen
	Halenberg
	Rosenberg
Münsterappel	Graukatz
Niederhausen an der Nahe	Graukatz
Niedermoschel	Geissenkopf
	Hahnhölle
	Layenberg
	Silberberg
Nussbaum	Höllenberg
	Rotfeld
	Sonnenberg
Oberhausen an der Nahe	Graukatz
Obermoschel	Geissenkopf
	Langhölle
	Schlossberg
	Silberberg
	Sonnenplätzchen
Oberndorf	Aspenberg
	Beutelstein
	Feuersteinrossel
	Weissenstein
Oberstreit	Auf dem Zimmerberg
Odernheim	Disibodenberg
	Hessweg
	Kapellenberg
	Kloster
	Monfort
	Weinsack
Raumbach	Schlossberg
	Schwalbennest
Rehborn	Hahn
	Herrenberg

Weinbauort (village)	*Einzellage (vineyard)*
Rehborn	Schikanenbuckel
Sobernheim	Domberg
	Marbach
Sobernheim-Steinhardt	Johannesberg
	Spitalberg
Staudernheim	Goldgrube
	Herrenberg
Unkenbach	Römerpfad
	Würzhölle
Waldböckelheim	Johannesberg
	Kastell
Weiler bei Monzingen	Heiligenberg
	Herrenzehntel
Winterborn	Graukatz

ROSENGARTEN: *Grosslage*

Bockenau	Geisberg
	Im Felseneck
	Im Neuberg
	Stromberg
Braunweiler	Hellenpfad
	Michaeliskapelle
	Schlossberg
	Wetterkreuz
Burgsponheim	Höllenpfad
	Pfaffenberg
	Schlossberg
Hüffelsheim	Gutenhölle
	Mönchberg
	Steyer
Mandel	Alte Römerstrasse
	Becherbrunnen
	Dellchen
	Palmengarten
	Schlossberg
Roxheim	Berg

Weinbauort (village)	Einzellage (vineyard)
Roxheim	Birkenberg
	Höllenpfad
	Hüttenberg
	Mühlenberg
	Sonnenberg
Rüdesheim	Goldgrube
	Wiesberg
St Katharinen	Fels
	Klostergarten
	Steinkreuz
Sponheim	Abtei
	Grafenberg
	Klostergarten
	Mühlberg
Weinsheim	Katergrube
	Kellerberg
	Steinkaut

CHAPTER 11

Rheinhessen (Hesse)

Area:	16,888 hectares
Average crop:	1,500,000 hectolitres
Types:	92 per cent white
	8 per cent red
Vines:	39 per cent Silvaner
	36 per cent Müller-Thurgau
	7 per cent Portugieser
	6 per cent Riesling

The wine-growing region of Rheinhessen lies between the Rhine and the Nahe, but to all intents and purposes it is a Rhine region. In effect, it is the district that lies north-east of a line from just south of Bingen to just south of Worms, with Mainz at its northernmost point.

It is dullish, undulating country, less attractive than Rheinpfalz, to the south, and consequently less visited by tourists.

The vine flourishes here, in rich soil and in a benign climate, and the wines are soft and bland, 'the most obvious and easy to know of all German growths', says Lichine.[1]

Only some twenty miles by thirty, the region produces very nearly as much wine as the Rheinpfalz, and exports more than any other region. The Silvaner was long the most widely grown grape here, but in this soil and climate its wine is bland

1. *Encyclopaedia of Wines and Spirits*, London, Cassell, 1975.

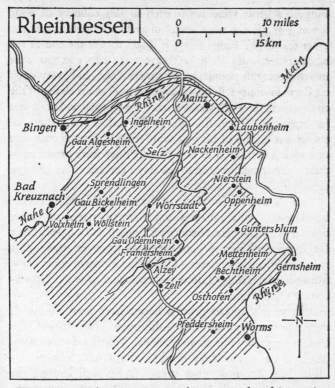

and lacking in character. Hence the increased and increasing importance of the Müller-Thurgau.

All Rheinhessen wines are fragrant, and sweetish to sweet: the best come from what is called 'the Rhine front' south of Mainz – Nackenheim, Nierstein and Oppenheim – where the Riesling grape (not widely planted in Rheinhessen), grown in lighter soil than other parts of the region, produces firm, full wines with a rich bouquet, outstanding dessert wines when late-gathered.

There are good wines, too, from across the peninsula, near

Bingen, a great wine town even in this country of wine towns – as great a wine town, indeed, as Rüdesheim, at the other end of the Rhine ferry. It is said that at the end of the nineteenth century there were 130 wine bars and 120 wine merchants for its population of a mere 6,000, and every book on German wines tells how, centuries ago, at a meeting of the city council, the Burgomaster asked for a pencil and none was forthcoming. When, though, at the end of the session, he pulled out bottles of his best wine from under the chair and asked for a corkscrew as many corkscrews were produced as there were councillors. So to this day a corkscrew is a 'Bingen pencil'.

Until the coming into force of the new wine law, two of the best-known generic names for German wines of rather ordinary quality were Niersteiner Domtal and Oppenheimer Goldberg. Such names were permitted to cover areas with a radius of fifteen kilometres – Niersteiner Domtals could come from vineyards thirty kilometres apart and so could Oppenheimer Goldbergs.

Such widely spread generic names have been abolished: there is now no Oppenheimer Goldberg, and Niersteiner Gutes Domtal, replacing Niersteiner Domtal, is restricted to Nierstein itself and the immediately neighbouring twelve villages.

Liebfraumilch is another matter. As is well known, the name came originally from the vineyards of the Liebfrauen-kirche, in Worms – vineyards that still exist. Eventually, the law allowed it to be applied to any Rhine wine – not necessarily from Rheinhessen – of good quality. This has been partly limited, partly extended, thus:

The name 'Liebfraumilch' can be used only for a QbA wine – not either a *Tafelwein* or a QmP wine – from Rhein-pfalz, Rheinhessen, Nahe or Rheingau – not from the Mittel-rhein or any other region.

It must be made from, and have the characteristics of, the

Riesling, Silvaner or Müller-Thurgau grape, but is not allowed to name it.

At the time of writing, discussions are still going on about Liebfraumilch – it is anomalous, for instance, that a wine made from a grape specified by law is forbidden by that same law to name it; and why, it is asked, should a wine blended from more than one region be a 'quality' wine? No other blend is granted such a distinction.

Meanwhile, shippers are relying more and more upon brand names to popularize and to sell their wines otherwise entitled to be called Liebfraumilch: Hanns Christof Wine, Blue Nun, Kellergeist and Three Crowns are among the names that come to mind.

Should the law be amended, and the name 'Liebfraumilch' confined to unblended wines from Rheinhessen, such wines will go on being sold as branded *Tafelwein*, without the word 'Liebfraumilch', relying on blending to maintain consistency of character. I was told at the house of Sichel Söhne, for instance, at Mainz, that their Blue Nun is usually a blend of Rheinhessen and Palatinate wines, but includes some from the Rheingau in years when such a blend lacks acidity.

Wine-snobs, and even unsnobbish keen amateurs of wine, look down their noses at wines labelled 'Liebfraumilch' whether or not they also carry a brand name.

This is unwise: Liebfraumilch is never a fine or a great hock, but good firms go to considerable trouble to maintain consistency of style in such wines, and the German wine law demands a minimum level of quality.

I have often been glad to find a Liebfraumilch from a named shipper in the wine-list of some modest Soho restaurant, or provincial railway hotel, where all else was unknown. I would know what I was getting if I ordered such a bottle – no great pleasurable surprise, certainly, but no shock of disappointment, either.

Although, after Liebfraumilch, the general names of Rheinhessen wines best known abroad are Niersteiner and Oppenheimer, I have learned from my German friends to look out for the wines of Nackenheim. They are occasionally to be found, at any rate in one or two London lists, such as that of O. W. Loeb of Jermyn Street, and they show the Hesse style at its best – soft and fruity yet far from heavy or bland.

THE VINEYARDS OF RHEINHESSEN

BINGEN (*Bereich*)

ABTEL: *Grosslage*

Weinbauort (*village*)	Einzellage (*vineyard*)
Appenheim	Daubhaus
	Drosselborn
	Eselspfad
	Hundertgulden
Gau-Algesheim	Goldberg
	Johannesberg
	Rothenberg
	St Laurenzikapelle
	Steinert
Nieder-Hilbersheim	Honigberg
	Steinacker
Ober-Hilbersheim	Mönchpforte
Partenheim	Sankt Georgen
	Steinberg
Sankt Johann	Geyersberg
	Klostergarten
	Steinberg
Sprendlingen	Hölle
	Honigberg
	Klostergarten
	Sonnenberg
	Wissberg

Weinbauort (village)	Einzellage (vineyard)
Wolfsheim	Götzenborn
	Osterberg
	Sankt Kathrin

ADELBERG: *Grosslage*

Armsheim	Geiersberg
	Goldstückchen
	Leckerberg
Bermersheim v. d. H.	Hildegardisberg
	Klosterberg
Bornheim	Hähnchen
	Hütte-Terrassen
	Kirchenstück
	Schönberg
Ensheim	Kachelberg
Erbes-Bürdesheim	Geisterberg
	Vogelsang
Flonheim	Bingerberg
	Klostergarten
	La Roche
	Pfaffenberg
	Rotenpfad
Lonsheim	Mandelberg
	Schönberg
Nack	Ahrenberg
Nieder-Weisen	Wingertsberg
Sulzheim	Greifenberg
	Honigberg
	Schildberg
Wendelsheim	Heiligenpfad
	Steigerberg
Wörrstadt	Kachelberg
	Rheingrafenberg

KAISERPFALZ: *Grosslage*

Weinbauort (village)	*Einzellage (vineyard)*
Bubenheim	Honigberg
	Kallenberg
Engelstadt	Adelpfad
	Römerberg
Gross-Winternheim	Bockstein
	Heilighäuschen
	Klosterbruder
	Schlossberg
Heidesheim	Geissberg
	Höllenberg
	Steinacker
Ingelheim	Burgberg
	Höllenweg
	Horn
	Kirchenstück
	Lottenstück
	Pares
	Rabenkopf
	Rheinhöhe
	Rotes Kreuz
	Schlossberg
	Schloss Westerhaus
	Sonnenberg
	Sonnenhang
	Steinacker
	Täuscherspfad
Jugenheim	Goldberg
	Hasensprung
	Heiligenhäuschen
	St Georgenberg
Schwabenheim	Klostergarten
	Schlossberg
	Sonnenberg
Wackernheim	Rabenkopf

Weinbauort (village)	*Einzellage (vineyard)*
Wackernheim	Schwalben
	Steinberg

KURFÜRSTENSTÜCK : *Grosslage*

Gau-Bickelheim	Bockshaut
	Kapelle
	Satıkopf
Gau-Weinheim	Geyersberg
	Kaisergarten
	Wissberg
Gumbsheim	Schlosshölle
Vendersheim	Goldberg
	Sonnenberg
Wallertheim	Heil
	Vogelsang

RHEINGRAFENSTEIN : *Grosslage*

Eckelsheim	Eselstreiber
	Kirchberg
	Sonnenköpfchen
Frei-Laubersheim	Fels
	Kirchberg
	Reichskeller
	Rheingrafenberg
Fürfeld	Eichelberg
	Kapellenberg
	Steige
Hackenheim	Galgenberg
	Gewürzgarten
	Kirchberg
	Klostergarten
	Sonnenberg
Neu-Bamberg	Eichelberg
	Heerkretz
	Kirschwingert
	Kletterberg

Weinbauort (village)	*Einzellage (vineyard)*
Pleitersheim	Sternberg
Siefersheim	Goldenes Horn
	Heerkretz
	Höllberg
	Martinsberg
Stein-Bockenheim	Sonnenberg
Tiefenthal	Graukatz
Volxheim	Alte Römerstrasse
	Liebfrau
	Mönchberg
Wöllstein	Affchen
	Haarberg-Katzensteg
	Hölle
	Ölberg
Wonsheim	Hölle
	Sonnenberg

SANKT ROCHUSKAPELLE: *Grosslage*

Aspisheim	Johannisberg
	Sonnenberg
Badenheim	Galgenberg
	Römerberg
Biebelsheim	Honigberg
	Kieselberg
Bingen	Bubenstück
	Kapellenberg
	Kirchberg
	Osterberg
	Pfarrgarten
	Rosengarten
	Scharlachberg
	Schelmenstück
	Schlossberg-Schwätzerchen
	Schwarzenberg
Dromersheim	Honigberg
	Kapellenberg

Weinbauort (village)	*Einzellage (vineyard)*
Dromersheim	Klosterweg
	Mainzerweg
Gensingen	Goldberg
Grolsheim	Ölberg
Horrweiler	Gewürzgärtchen
	Goldberg
Ockenheim	Hockenmühle
	Klosterweg
	Kreuz
	Laberstall
	St Jakobsberg
	Schönhölle
Pfaffen-Schwabenheim	Hölle
	Mandelbaum
	Sonnenberg
Sponsheim	Palmenstein
Welgesheim	Kirchgärtchen
Zotzenheim	Johannisberg
	Klostergarten
	Sackträger
	Schützenhütte
	Zuckerberg

NIERSTEIN (*Bereich*)

AUFLANGEN: *Grosslage*

Nierstein	Bergkirche
	Glöck
	Heiligenbaum
	Kranzberg
	Ölberg
	Orbel
	Schloss Schwabsburg
	Zehnmorgen

DOMHERR: *Grosslage*

Weinbauort (village)	*Einzellage (vineyard)*
Budenheim	sites not chosen
Essenheim	Römerberg
	Teufelspfad
Gabsheim	Dornpfad
	Kirchberg
	Rosengarten
Klein-Winternheim	Geiershöll
	Herrgottshaus
	Villenkeller
Mainz-Drais	sites not chosen
Mainz-Finthen	sites not chosen
Ober-Olm	Kapellenberg
Saulheim	Haubenberg
	Heiligenhaus
	Hölle
	Pfaffengarten
	Probstey
	Schlossberg
Schornsheim	Mönchspfad
	Ritterberg
	Sonnenhang
Stadecken-Elsheim	Blume
	Bockstein
	Lenchen
	Spitzberg
	Tempelchen
Udenheim	Goldberg
	Kirchberg
	Sonnenberg

GÜLDENMORGEN: *Grosslage*

Dienheim	Falkenberg
	Herrenberg
	Höhlchen

Weinbauort (village)	*Einzellage (vineyard)*
Dienheim	Kreuz
	Siliusbrunnen
	Tafelstein
Oppenheim	Daubhaus
	Gutleuthaus
	Herrenberg
	Kreuz

GUTES DOMTAL: *Grosslage*

Dalheim	Altdörr
	Kranzberg
	Steinberg
Dexheim	Doktor
Friesenheim	Altdörr
	Bergpfad
	Knopf
Hahnheim	Knopf
	Moosberg
Köngernheim	Goldgrube
Lörzweiler	Königstuhl
Mommenheim	Kloppenberg
	Osterberg
	Silbergrube
Nackenheim	Schmittskapellchen
Nieder-Olm	Goldberg
	Klosterberg
	Sonnenberg
Nierstein	Pfaffenkappe
Selzen	Gottesgarten
	Osterberg
	Rheinpforte
Sörgenloch	Moosberg
Undenheim	Goldberg
Weinolsheim	Hohberg
	Kehr
Zornheim	Dachgewann

Weinbauort (village)	Einzellage (vineyard)
Zornheim	Güldenmorgen
	Mönchbäumchen
	Pilgerweg
	Vogelsang

KRÖTENBRUNNEN: *Grosslage*

Alsheim	Goldberg
Dienheim	Herrengarten
	Paterhof
	Schloss
Dolgesheim	Kreuzberg
	Schützenhütte
Eich	Goldberg
Eimsheim	Hexelberg
	Römerschanze
	Sonnenhang
Gimbsheim	Liebfrauenthal
	Sonnenweg
Guntersblum	Eiserne Hand
	Sankt Julianenbrunnen
	Sonnenberg
	Sonnenhang
	Steinberg
Hillesheim	Altenberg
	Sonnheil
Ludwigshöhe	Honigberg
Mettenheim	Goldberg
Oppenheim	Herrengarten
	Paterhof
	Schloss
	Schlossberg
Ülversheim	Aulenberg
	Schloss
Wintersheim	Frauengarten

PETERSBERG: *Grosslage*

Weinbauort (village)	*Einzellage (vineyard)*
Albig	Homberg
	Hundskopf
	Schloss Hammerstein
Bechtolsheim	Homberg
	Klosterberg
	Sonnenberg
	Wingertstor
Biebelnheim	Pilgerstein
	Rosenberg
Framersheim	Hornberg
	Kreuzweg
	Zechberg
Gau-Heppenheim	Pfarrgarten
	Schlossberg
Gau-Odernheim	Fuchsloch
	Herrgottspfad
	Ölberg
	Vogelsang
Spiesheim	Osterberg

REHBACH: *Grosslage*

Nackenheim	Rothenberg
Nierstein	Brudersberg
	Goldene Luft
	Hipping
	Pettenthal

RHEINBLICK: *Grosslage*

Alsheim	Fischerpfad
	Frühmesse
	Römerberg
	Sonnenberg
Dorn-Dürkheim	Hasensprung
	Römerberg

Weinbauort (village)	Einzellage (vineyard)
Mettenheim	Michelsberg
	Schlossberg

SANKT ALBAN: *Grosslage*

Bodenheim	Burgweg
	Ebersberg
	Heitersbrünnchen
	Hoch
	Kapelle
	Kreuzberg
	Leidhecke
	Mönchspfad
	Reichsritterstift
	Silberberg
	Westrum
Gau-Bischofsheim	Glockenberg
	Herrnberg
	Kellersberg
	Pfaffenweg
Harxheim	Börnchen
	Lieth
	Schlossberg
Lörzweiler	Hohberg
	Ölgild
Mainz	Edelmann
	Hüttberg
	Johannisberg
	Kirchenstück
	Klosterberg
	Sand
	Weinkeller

SPIEGELBERG: *Grosslage*

Nackenheim	Engelsberg
Nierstein	Bildstock
	Brückchen

Weinbauort (village)	Einzellage (vineyard)
Nierstein	Ebersberg
	Findling
	Hölle
	Kirchplatte
	Klostergarten
	Paterberg
	Rosenberg
	Schloss Hohenrechen

VOGELSGÄRTEN: *Grosslage*

Guntersblum	Authental
	Bornpfad
	Himmelthal
	Kreuzkapelle
	Steig-Terrassen
Ludwigshöhe	Teufelskopf

WONNEGAU (*Bereich*)

BERGKLOSTER: *Grosslage*

Bermersheim	Hasenlauf
Eppelsheim	Felsen
Esselborn	Goldberg
Flomborn	Feuerberg
	Goldberg
Gundersheim	Höllenbrand
	Königstuhl
Gundheim	Hungerbiene
	Mandelbrunnen
	Sonnenberg
Hangen-Weisheim	Sommerwende
Westhofen	Aulerde
	Benn
	Brunnenhäuschen
	Kirchspiel
	Morstein

Weinbauort (village)	*Einzellage (vineyard)*
Westhofen	Rotenstein
	Steingrube

BURG RODENSTEIN: *Grosslage*

Bermersheim/Worms	Seilgarten
Flörsheim-Dalsheim	Bürgel
	Frauenberg
	Goldberg
	Hubacker
	Sauloch
	Steig
Mörstadt	Katzebuckel
	Nonnengarten
Ober-Flörsheim	Blücherpfad
	Herrenberg

DOMBLICK: *Grosslage*

Hohen-Sülzen	Kirchenstück
	Sonnenberg
Mölsheim	Silberberg
	Zellerweg am schw. Herrgott
Monsheim	Rosengarten
	Silberberg
Offstein	Engelsberg
	Schlossgarten
Wachenheim	Horn
	Rotenberg

GOTTESHILFE: *Grosslage*

Bechtheim	Geyersberg
	Rosengarten
	Stein
Osthofen	Goldberg
	Hasenbiss
	Leckzapfen
	Neuberg

LIEBFRAUENMORGEN: *Grosslage*

Weinbauort (village)	*Einzellage (vineyard)*
Worms	Affenberg
	Am Heiligen Häuschen
	Bildstock
	Burgweg
	Goldberg
	Goldpfad
	Hochberg
	Kapellenstück
	Klausenberg
	Kreuzblick
	Lerchelsberg
	Liebfrauenstift-Kirchenstück
	Nonnenwingert
	Remeyerhof
	Rheinberg
	Römersteg
	Sankt Annaberg
	St Cyriakusstift
	St Georgenberg
	Schneckenberg

PILGERPFAD: *Grosslage*

Bechtheim	Hasensprung
	Heiligkreuz
Dittelsheim-Hessloch	Edle Weingärten
	Geiersberg
	Kloppberg
	Leckerberg
	Liebfrauenberg
	Mönchhube
	Mondschein
	Pfaffenmütze
Frettenheim	Heil

Weinbauort (village)	*Einzellage (vineyard)*
Monzernheim	Goldberg
	Steinböhl
Osthofen	Kirchberg
	Klosterberg
	Liebenberg
	Rheinberg

SYBILLENSTEIN: *Grosslage*

Alzey	Kapellenberg
	Pfaffenhalde
	Römerberg
	Rotenfels
	Wartberg
Bechenheim	Fröhlich
Dautenheim	Himmelacker
Freimersheim	Frankenstein
Heimersheim	Sonnenberg
Mauchenheim	Sioner Klosterberg
Offenheim	Mandelberg
Wahlheim	Schelmen
Weinheim	Heiliger Blutberg
	Hölle
	Kapellenberg
	Kirchenstück
	Mandelberg

CHAPTER 12

Hessische Bergstrasse

Area:	272 hectares
Average crop:	28,000 hectolitres
Type:	Virtually all white; a very little pink
Vines:	53 per cent Riesling
	18 per cent Silvaner
	18 per cent Müller-Thurgau
	6 per cent Ruländer

When I last visited the wine-growing areas of Germany, at the end of 1975, to visit regions I did not know, my friends in the Rheingau expressed surprise that I should trouble to make a journey even of a mere forty minutes or so by autobahn to the Hessische Bergstrasse.

It was such a small region, they said – the smallest in Germany by a long chalk: it was so cut off; it was so unimportant; and for the purposes of the wine law it might just as well have been thrown in with Rheinhessen.

What is more, they said, nobody knew or cared anything about its wines – except, they supposed, the local people themselves.

They need not have excluded the locals. We arrived at Bensheim, the sizeable, sprawling town that is the metropolis of the Bergstrasse, and sought guidance at the leading hotel, which advertised itself also as a wine-house.

The only German wines in the list (there were a couple of French wines) were nine from the Hessische Bergstrasse itself and two from Rheinhessen. We asked the waiter about them: he summoned the owner. Could he, perhaps, recommend one of the local wines, and tell us anything about them?

Well no, he didn't know much about wine, *meine Herren*, but he was sure we would be pleased with whatever we chose: everything was good.

Had he any idea why the Bergstrasse, small and little-known as it was, had been granted independence as a region by the German wine law?

No idea at all: could it, he mused, be because the Bergstrasse wines were stronger than those from across the river? No, he didn't know: it was an idea that had just occurred to him . . .

He could not have known less about the wine he served had he been a Turkish-Cypriot waiter in a Soho Chinese restaurant: he could not have cared less about what he sold to his customers had he been a waitress in a British Rail buffet.

But he was a good deal more civil. He did not get so carried away by anxiety to please as to offer us a glass of wine on the house, but he did give us the addresses of his three suppliers: he was sure any of them would be glad to help.

He knew as little about his fellow-townsmen as about his wines.

We arrived at the municipal wine-cellars at not quite half-past four: the office was closed. As we were turning away, two men emerged from the cellars, and made for their motor-cycles in the yard.

We asked for a word with them, and explained why. Sorry, they said, it was going-home time.

My companion said that perhaps he had not made himself clear: we had come especially from England to write a book about German wines. In that case, said the cellermen, perhaps we would come back tomorrow.

One last throw: could they direct us to the state cellars? Well yes, they said, already a little put out by having been held up for a good ten minutes: well yes, they said pointedly, but *they* would have gone home, too . . .

*

As will have been realized, a good deal of the Hessische Bergstrasse wine is produced by municipally owned and state-owned vineyards – the latter from former Prussian state domains.[1]

Indeed, at a wide-ranging tasting arranged for us in Mainz, Herr Riquet Hess of Sichel Söhne, having learned of our lack of luck in the Bergstrasse itself, managed to find us a 1971 Heppenheimer Zentgericht Riesling Auslese bearing the handsome label common to the state domains. It showed well enough in good company – it was virtually impossible to make a mediocre wine anywhere in Germany in 1971 – though without the fullness or flavour of the Pfalz and Rheinhessen wines at the same tasting, and with nothing of the balance of fruit and acidity, and therefore of the subtlety, of the Rheingaus.

*

The Bergstrasse vineyards are on the lower westward-facing slopes of the steep but rounded, thickly wooded hump of the Odenwald, interspersed with small orchards, modest market-gardens, and meadows in which munch the black-and-white cattle of the region.

Of the wines, I know little, and even the little I know is more than is known even by many members of the German wine trade, or by *cognoscenti* in near-by parts of this handsome countryside.

Apart from the 1971 Heppenheimer I have mentioned, which must be regarded as outstanding by local standards, I have drunk in Bensheim a pleasant dry, very pale pink *Weissherbst*,[2] cleaner to the palate than many a French *rosé*, though without much character, and I gather that, unlike other regions, the Hessische Bergstrasse thinks more highly of its few Ruländer than of its many Riesling wines. At any rate, it charges more.

1. See p. 49.
2. See p. 62.

Generally speaking, the Hessische Bergstrasse wines are mild and bland, and they are all drunk on the spot – by the few German and fewer foreign visitors to this charming country of woodland, meadow and trim little upland towns, flirtatious with flowery window-boxes, and by the locals themselves, hurrying home for tea at twenty to five.

THE VINEYARDS OF HESSISCHE BERGSTRASSE
STARKENBURG (*Bereich*)

ROTT: *Grosslage*

Weinbauort (*village*)	*Einzellage* (*vineyard*)
Auerbach	Fürstenlager
	Höllberg
Schönberg	Herrnwingert

Not yet assigned a *Grosslage*:

Seeheim	Mundklingen
Zwingenberg	Alte Burg
	Steingeröll

SCHLOSSBERG: *Grosslage*

Heppenheim (including Erbach and Hambach)	Eckweg
	Guldenzoll
	Maiberg
	Steinkopf
	Stemmler
	Zentgericht

WOLFSMAGEN: *Grosslage*

Bensheim	Hemsberg
	Kalkgasse
	Kirchberg
	Paulus
	Streichling

UMSTADT (*Bereich*)

Weinbauort (village)	*Einzellage (vineyard)*
Dietzenbach	Wingertsberg
Gross Umstadt	Herrnberg
	Stachelberg
	Steingerück
Klein-Umstadt	
Rossdorf	Rossberg

Rheinpfalz

Area:	18,621 hectares
Average crop:	1,700,000 hectolitres
Types:	84 per cent white
	16 per cent red
Vines:	33 per cent Silvaner
	23 per cent Müller-Thurgau
	16 per cent Portugieser
	14 per cent Riesling

This is not only the biggest wine-growing region of Germany, but almost always produces the biggest yield per hectare.[1]

Unlike other regions, strung along the Rhine, the Mosel or the Neckar, the vineyards of the Palatinate stand back, ten miles or so to the west, from the river, along the Deutsche Weinstrasse – the German Wine Road.

From the great eagle-topped Weintor – Wine Gate – at Schweigen, on the French frontier, near Wissembourg, the road winds north for almost fifty miles to the southern tip of Rheinhessen through a richly fertile plain, sheltered on the west and the north by the Haardt mountains, a northern extension of the Vosges of Alsace.

In many places along the road one is reminded of the Médoc. The vineyards stretch on either side – a green ribbon varying

1. The only recent exception was in 1971, when the Mosel-Saar-Ruwer produced 104 hectolitres per hectare to the Rheinpfalz's 87·6.

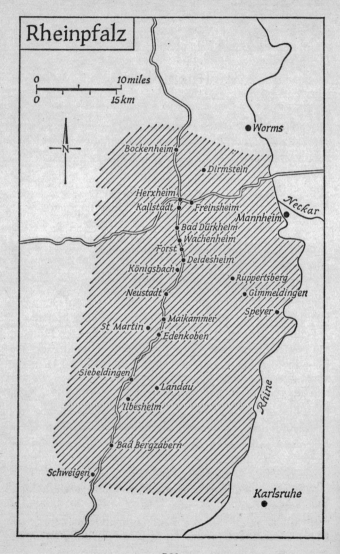

Rheinpfalz

0   10 miles
0   15 km

N

Worms

Bockenheim

Dirmstein

Herxheim
Kallstadt   Freinsheim
Neckar
Mannheim
Bad Dürkheim
Wachenheim
Forst
Deidesheim
Königsbach
Ruppertsberg
Neustadt
Gimmeldingen
Speyer
Maikammer
St Martin
Edenkoben
Siebeldingen
Landau
Ilbesheim
Bad Bergzabern
Rhine
Schweigen
Karlsruhe

from a mile to three miles in width, with a glimpse of the Rhine to the east, as one glimpses the Gironde across the vineyards of Latour, say, but on the west, instead of the pine forests of the Landes, the wooded crest of the Haardt.

Of all the wine-growing regions of Germany, only the Rheingau has so mild – usually even milder – a climate, and the Rheingau is a mere sixth of the area: this is fig and almond country as well as a vast vineyard. Rainfall is low, sunshine is considerable – and the soil is rich. Naturally, the wines of the Palatinate are full and soft, not so fragrant as the wines of the Rheingau or the Mosel, but the sweetest of the sweet when the finest are late-gathered. A high proportion of them, though, are pretty simple wines, drunk first immediately after the vintage, before they have properly fermented, half fruit-juice, half wine, cloudy in the glass, sweet and heady.

Then as *Schoppenwein*, open wine, heady still, but true wine now; and even when bottled, a great deal of the Palatinate wine is drunk very young – heavy, sweet or at any rate sweetish. 'It goes into your legs', I have heard a Rheingauer say of it.

Three clearly defined districts make up the Palatinate.

From the Wine Gate on the French frontier to Neustadt is the Upper Haardt, producing more than half of the region's wines, for although their quality is improving, the emphasis is still on quantity: there are vineyards here that regularly make record yields per hectare.

It is open-wine country, and pleasant country to drink it in – very like its southern neighbour, Alsace, with its picture-postcard villages and welcoming wine-bars.

Then, from Neustadt to Dackenheim, we are in the Middle Haardt, the district whence come the best wines of the Palatinate and, in the middle of the middle, so to speak, the small group of villages that produce the finest of all: Forst, Deidesheim, Ruppertsberg, Koenigsbach and Wachenheim.

Here the proportion of Rieslings is much higher than elsewhere in the region, and three great growing families – Bassermann-Jordan, von Buhl and Bürklin-Wolf – dedicate themselves to producing wines that show the Palatinate style at its best – full but balanced – and especially great sweet late-gathered wines, as rich as any in Germany.

So, although the Palatinate as a whole region is not in the same class as the Rheingau, say, or the Mosel for its general level of quality, a combination of one of these growers' names with any of the villages mentioned in the previous paragraph will indicate a wine of great character, full and fruity, yet well balanced. Such wines are fairly widely available in the better British and American wine merchants' lists, and in some restaurants. But they are never – for they cannot be – cheap.

Other villages in this Middle Haardt region produce wines of considerable quality, and around the sizeable town of Neustadt and the pretty spa, Bad Dürkheim, there is a modest amount of red wine grown – modest in quality as well as in quantity.

This is a region of fêtes and galas – there is an annual Sausage Fair at Bad Dürkheim, a frolicsome Billy-Goat Auction every Whitsuntide at Deidesheim, an Almond Blossom Festival each March at Gimmeldingen, a Wine Festival at Neustadt and another at Edenkoben, where they also bless the chestnuts. Others, too – all good excuses for plenty of wine-swilling, as if excuse were needed.

North of the Middle Haardt is one more stretch of wine-growing, the northern third of the Palatinate, from Herxheim, near Bad Dürkheim, to the southern edge of the Rheinhessen region, at Zell (not to be confused with the Zell on the Mosel).

This is the smallest of the three districts of the Palatinate, and the least distinguished: with rare exceptions, its wines are bland and soft, without the body and character of their neighbours to the south.

Throughout the region there are big cooperatives, the wines of which are worth seeking out: methods are modern, controls are strict, and standards are high.

There is a Palatinate wine museum at Speyer, with an English-speaking guide.

THE VINEYARDS OF RHEINPFALZ

MITTELHAARDT-DEUTSCHE WEINSTRASSE
(*Bereich*)

FEUERBERG: *Grosslage*

Weinbauort (village)	Einzellage (vineyard)
Bad Dürkheim	Herrenmorgen
	Nonnengarten
	Steinberg
Bobenheim am Berg	Kieselberg
	Ohligpfad
Ellerstadt	Bubeneck
	Dickkopp
	Sonnenberg
Gönnheim	Martinshöhe
Kallstadt	Annaberg
	Kreidkeller
Weisenheim am Berg	Vogelsang

GRAFENSTÜCK: *Grosslage*

Bockenheim	Burggarten
	Goldgrube
	Hassmannsberg
	Heiligenkirche
	Klosterschaffnerei
	Schlossberg
	Sonnenberg
	Vogelsang

Weinbauort (village)	*Einzellage (vineyard)*
Kindenheim	Burgweg
	Katzenstein
	Sonnenberg
	Vogelsang
Obrigheim	Benn
	Hochgericht
	Mandelpfad
	Rosengarten
	Schloss
	Sonnenberg

HOCHMESS: *Grosslage*

Bad Dürkheim	Hochbenn
	Michelsberg
	Rittergarten
	Spielberg
Ungstein	Michelsberg

HÖLLENPFAD: *Grosslage*

Battenberg	Schlossberg
Grünstadt	Bergel
	Goldberg
	Honigsack
	Hütt
	Klostergarten
	Röth
	St Stephan
	Schloss
Kleinkarlbach	Frauenländchen
	Herrenberg
	Herrgottsacker
	Kieselberg
	Senn
Mertesheim	St Martinskreuz
Neuleiningen	Feuermännchen

Weinbauort (village)	*Einzellage (vineyard)*
Neuleiningen	Schlossberg
	Sonnenberg

HOFSTÜCK: *Grosslage*

Deidesheim	Nonnenstück
Ellerstadt	Kirchenstück
Friedelsheim	Gerümpel
	Rosengarten
Gönnheim	Klostergarten
	Mandelgarten
	Sonnenberg
Hochdorf-Assenheim	Fuchsloch
Meckenheim	Neuberg
	Spielberg
	Wolfsdarm
Niederkirchen	Klostergarten
	Osterbrunnen
	Schlossberg
Rödersheim-Gronau	Fuchsloch
Ruppertsberg	Gaisböhl
	Hoheburg
	Linsenbusch
	Nussbien
	Reiterpfad
	Spiess

HONIGSÄCKEL: *Grosslage*

Ungstein	Herrenberg
	Nussriegel
	Weilberg

KOBNERT: *Grosslage*

Dackenheim	Kapellgarten
	Liebesbrunnen
	Mandelröth
Erpolzheim	Kirschgarten

Weinbauort (village)	Einzellage (vineyard)
Freinsheim	Musikantenbuckel
	Oschelskopf
	Schwarzes Kreuz
Herxheim/Berg	Himmelreich
	Honigsack
	Kirchenstück
Kallstadt	Kronenberg
	Steinacker
Leistadt	Herzfeld
	Kalkofen
	Kirchenstück
Ungstein	Bettelhaus
	Osterberg
Weisenheim am Berg	Mandelgarten
	Sonnenberg

MARIENGARTEN: *Grosslage*

Deidesheim	Grainhübel
	Herrgottsacker
	Hohenmorgen
	Kalkofen
	Kieselberg
	Langenmorgen
	Leinhöhle
	Mäushöhle
	Paradiesgarten
Forst	Elster
	Freundstück
	Jesuitengarten
	Kirchenstück
	Musenhang
	Pechstein
	Ungeheuer
Wachenheim	Altenburg
	Belz
	Böhlig

Weinbauort (village)	*Einzellage (vineyard)*
Wachenheim	Gerümpel
	Goldbächel
	Rechbächel

MEERSPINNE: *Grosslage*

Gimmeldingen	Biengarten
	Kapellenberg
	Mandelgarten
	Schlössel
Haardt	Bürgergarten
	Herrenletten
	Herzog
	Mandelring
Königsbach	Idig
	Jesuitengarten
	Ölberg
	Reiterpfad
Mussbach	Bischofsweg
	Eselshaut
	Glockenzehnt
	Johannitergarten
	Kurfürst
	Spiegel
Neustadt an der Weinstrasse	Mönchgarten

PFAFFENGRUND: *Grosslage*

Diedesfeld	Berg
Duttweiler	Kalkberg
	Kreuzberg
	Mandelberg
Geinsheim	Gässel
Hambach	Römerbrunnen
Lachen-Speyerdorf	Kroatenpfad
	Langenstein
	Lerchenböhl

REBSTÖCKEL: *Grosslage*

Weinbauort (village)	*Einzellage (vineyard)*
Diedesfeld	Johanniskirchel
	Ölgässel
	Paradies
Hambach	Feuer
	Kaiserstuhl
	Kirchberg
	Schlossberg
Neustadt an der Weinstrasse	Erkenbrecht
	Grain

ROSENBÜHL: *Grosslage*

Erpolzheim	Goldberg
	Keiselberg
Freinsheim	Goldberg
Lambsheim	Burgweg
Weisenheim/Sand	Altenberg
	Burgweg
	Goldberg
	Hahnen
	Halde
	Hasenzeile

SAUMAGEN: *Grosslage*

Kallstadt	Horn
	Kirchenstück
	Nill

SCHENKENBÖHL: *Grosslage*

Bad Dürkheim	Abtsfronhof
	Fronhof
	Fuchsmantel
Wachenheim	Fuchsmantel
	Königswingert
	Mandelgarten

Weinbauort (village)	*Einzellage (vineyard)*
Wachenheim	Odinstal
	Schlossberg

SCHNEPFENFLUG VOM ZELLERTAL: *Grosslage*

Albisheim	Heiligenborn
Bolanden	Schlossberg
Bubenheim	Hahnenkamm
Einselthum	Klosterstüch
	Kreuzberg
Gauersheim	Goldloch
Immesheim	Sonnenstück
Kerzenheim	Esper
Kirchheimbolanden	Schlossgarten
Morschheim	Im Heubusch
Niefernheim	Königsweg
	Kreuzberg
Ottersheim/Zellerthal	Bräunersberg
Rittersheim	Am hohen Stein
Rüssingen	Breinsberg
Stetten	Heilighäuschen
Zell	Klosterstück
	Königsweg
	Kreuzberg
	Schwarzer Herrgott

SCHNEPFENFLUG AN DER WEINSTRASSE: *Grosslage*

Deidesheim	Letten
Forst	Bischofsgarten
	Stift
	Süsskopf
Friedelsheim	Bischofsgarten
	Kreuz
	Schlossgarten
Wachenheim	Bischofsgarten
	Luginsland

SCHWARZERDE: *Grosslage*

Weinbauort (village)	*Einzellage (vineyard)*
Bisserheim	Goldberg
	Held
	Orlenberg
	Steig
Dirmstein	Herrgottsacker
	Jesuitenhofgarten
	Mandelpfad
Gerolsheim	Klosterweg
	Lerchenspiel
Grosskarlbach	Burgweg
	Osterberg
Grossniedesheim	Schafberg
Hessheim	Lange Els
Heuchelheim/Frankenthal	Steinkopf
Kirchheim	Geisskopf
	Kreuz
	Römerstrasse
	Steinacker
Kleinniedesheim	Schlossgarten
	Vorderberg
Laumersheim	Kirschgarten
	Mandelberg
	Sonnengarten
Obersülzen	Schnepp

SÜDLICHE WEINSTRASSE (*Bereich*)

BISCHOFSKREUZ: *Grosslage*

Böchingen	Rosenkranz
Burrweiler	Altenforst
	St Annaberg
	Schäwer
	Schlossgarten
Dammheim	Höhe

Weinbauort (village)	Einzellage (vineyard)
Flemlingen	Herrenbuckel
	Vogelsprung
	Zechpeter
Gleisweiler	Hölle
Knöringen	Hohenrain
Nussdorf	Herrenberg
	Kaiserberg
	Kirchenstück
Roschbach	Rosenkränzel
	Simonsgarten
Walsheim	Forstweg
	Silberberg

GUTTENBERG: *Grosslage*

Bad Bergzabern	Wonneberg
Dierbach	Kirchhöh
Dörrenbach	Wonneberg
Freckenfeld	Gräfenberg
Kandel	Galgenberg
Kapsweyher	Lerchenberg
Minfeld	Herrenberg
Niederotterbach	Eselsbuckel
Oberotterbach	Sonnenberg
Schweigen-Rechtenbach	Sonnenberg
Schweighofen	Sonnenberg
	Wolfsberg
Steinfeld	Herrenwingert
Vollmersweiler	Krapfenberg

HERRLICH: *Grosslage*

Eschbach	Hasen
Göcklingen	Kaiserberg
Herxheim bei Landau	Engelsberg
Herxheimweyher	Am Gaisberg
Ilbesheim	Rittersberg
Impflingen	Abtsberg

Weinbauort (village)	Einzellage (vineyard)
Inshçim	Schäfergarten
Leinsweiler	Sonnenberg
Mörzheim	Pfaffenberg
Rohrbach	Schäfergarten
Wollmesheim	Mütterle

KLOSTER LIEBFRAUENBERG : *Grosslage*

Bad Bergzabern	Altenberg
Barbelroth	Kirchberg
Billigheim-Ingenheim	Mandelpfad
	Pfaffenberg
	Rosenberg
	Sauschwänzel
	Steingebiss
	Venusbuckel
Gleiszellen-Gleishorbach	Frühmess
	Kirchberg
Göcklingen	Herrenpfad
Hergersweiler	Narrenberg
Heuchelheim-Klingen	Herrenpfad
Kapellen-Drusweiler	Rosengarten
Klingenmünster	Maria Magdalena
Niederhorbach	Silberberg
Oberhausen	Frohnwingert
Pleisweiler-Oberhofen	Schlossberg
Rohrbach	Mandelpfad
Steinweiler	Rosenberg
Winden	Narrenberg

KÖNIGSGARTEN : *Grosslage*

Albersweiler	Kirchberg
	Latt
Arzheim	Rosenberg
	Seligmacher
Birkweiler	Kastanienbusch
	Mandelberg

Weinbauort (village)	Einzellage (vineyard)
Birkweiler	Rosenberg
Frankweiler	Biengarten
	Kalkgrube
Godramstein	Klostergarten
	Münzberg
Landau	Altes Löhl
Ranschbach	Seligmacher
Siebeldingen	Im Sonnenschein
	Mönchspfad
	Rosenberg

MANDELHÖHE: *Grosslage*

Kirrweiler	Mandelberg
	Oberschloss
	Römerweg
Maikammer	Heiligenberg
	Immengarten
	Kirchenstück
Maikammer-Alsterweiler	Kapellenberg

ORDENSGUT: *Grosslage*

Edesheim	Forst
	Mandelhang
	Rosengarten
	Schloss
Hainfeld	Kapelle
	Kirchenstück
	Letten
Rhodt	Klosterpfad
	Rosengarten
	Schlossberg
Weyher	Heide
	Michelsberg

SCHLOSS LUDWIGSHÖHE: *Grosslage*

Weinbauort (village)	*Einzellage (vineyard)*
Edenkoben	Bergel
	Blücherhöhe
	Heidegarten
	Heilig Kreuz
	Kastaniengarten
	Kirchberg
	Klostergarten
	Mühlberg
	Schwarzer Letten
St Martin	Baron
	Kirchberg
	Zitadelle

TRAPPENBERG: *Grosslage*

Altdorf	Gottesacker
	Hochgericht
Bellheim	Gollenberg
Böbingen	Ortelberg
Bornheim	Neuberg
Essingen	Osterberg
	Rossberg
	Sonnenberg
Freimersheim	Bildberg
Gross u. Kleinfischlingen	Kirchberg
Hochstadt	Rotenberg
Knittelsheim	Gollenberg
Lustadt	Klostergarten
Ottersheim	Kahlenberg
Römerberg	Alter Berg
	Narrenberg
	Schlittberg
Schwegenheim	Bründelsberg
Venningen	Doktor
Weingarten	Schlossberg
Zeiskam	Klostergarten

CHAPTER 14

Baden

Area:	9,525 hectares
Average crop:	700,000 hectolitres
Types:	78 per cent white
	22 per cent red
Vines:	26 per cent Müller-Thurgau
	22 per cent Spätburgunder
	13 per cent Ruländer
	13 per cent Gutedel
	7 per cent Silvaner
	7 per cent Riesling
	4 per cent Weissburgunder
	2 per cent Traminer

This is the south-westernmost corner of Germany, facing Switzerland southwards across Lake Constance (Bodensee) and the Rhine until the river makes its right-angled turn at Basle, and then facing Alsace across the Rhine to the west.

Baden was Germany's greatest wine-producing area until about 1870, when the phylloxera brought cultivation down by about a half; then, just before the last war, a new wine law ordained the uprooting of hybrid vines for the sake of quality.[1] Baden had relied more than any other region on its

1. A hybrid is a cross between the 'noble' European grape, *Vitis vinifera*, and an American species; it is outlawed in Germany and is not permitted in France or Italy for wines of *appellation*, VDQS or DOC

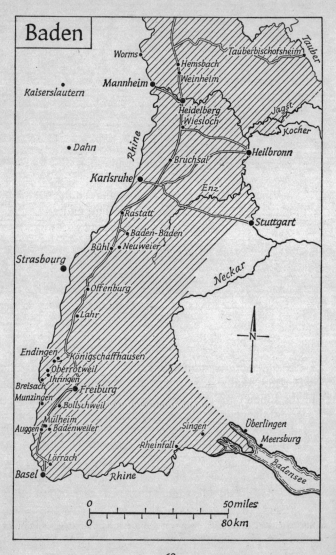

Baden

Worms
Kaiserslautern
Hemsbach
Tauberbischofsheim
Tauber
Weinheim
Mannheim
Heidelberg
Wiesloch
Jagst
Rhine
Dahn
Kocher
Bruchsal
Heilbronn
Karlsruhe
Enz
Rastatt
Stuttgart
Baden-Baden
Bühl
Neuweier
Strasbourg
Neckar
Offenburg
Lahr
N
Endingen
Königschaffhausen
Oberrotweil
Ihringen
Breisach
Freiburg
Munzingen
Bollschweil
Mülheim
Singen
Überlingen
Auggen
Badenweiler
Meersburg
Rheinfall
Lörrach
Basel
Rhine
Badensee

0   50 miles
0   80 km

168

hybrids, and not only was the area under vines further reduced by about a quarter, but production went down as high-quality replaced high-quantity varieties.

Now, wine-growing is nothing like so general as in other regions; it is concentrated in separate districts notably different from each other; and, as it is largely in the hands of smallholders, 90 per cent of Baden wine comes from co-operatives.

The *Föhn* – the sirocco-like south wind that sweeps across Lake Constance – turns milk sour and women even more so, but ripens the Ruländer (Pinot Gris) and Gewürztraminer grapes on the northern shore. Their white wines in consequence are soft and sweetish; but there is also a local speciality, the *Weissherbst*, which is what the French would call a *blanc de noirs*, made by taking the must away almost immediately from the skins of the black Spätburgunder grape (see page 56), to produce a white wine tinged only very slightly with pink – a pretty wine to drink in the pretty lakeside restaurants.

Downstream, they grow light, fresh white wines from the Gutedel grape (which in France and Switzerland is the Chasselas) in an area between the handsome city of Freiburg and the point, opposite Basle, where the Rhine turns north. This is the Markgräflerland, or Markgräfschaft.

Between Freiburg and the Rhine the hump of the Kaiserstuhl heaves itself out of the plain: its rich volcanic soil gives body to some of the best of Baden's wines – some reds, from the Spätburgunder; some whites, all with more depth to them than those of the Bodensee and the Markgräflerland.

The Breisgau wines, from north of Freiburg, are less distinguished except for the *Weissherbste*, which seem to have more backbone to them than those of the lakeside.

---

status. The *grafting* of *Vitis vinifera* on to American roots is, of course, not only permitted , but almost universal.

From here to beyond delightfully elegant Baden-Baden is the Ortenau region, merging into the Badische-Bergstrasse. Between the thickly wooded heights of the Black Forest and the Rhine grow some elegant whites (many from the Riesling, here called the Klingelberger) and some reasonably drinkable reds. Many of the whites are dry: the wine-list of Brenner's Park-Hotel at Baden-Baden lists twenty-seven Baden whites before even reaching the late-gathered group and no fewer than eleven are marked 'trocken'.

This is the area in which to look for the Mauerwein Rieslings, from around Neuweier – pleasantly crisp and dry and, along with a few wines from Baden's Tauber valley, the only wines permitted by German law, as a gesture to long tradition, to be put up in the flagon-shaped *Bocksbeutel* otherwise restricted to the wines of Franconia.

Another oddity of the region is the red Affenthaler, from a valley near Baden-Baden called Ave Thal, which is to say, because of a monastery that once stood there, Ave-Maria valley. The German language pronounces 'v' as 'f': the valley village became known as Affenthal, and as in German an *Affe* is a monkey the growers took to selling their wine in a bottle embossed with the figure of a monkey. A good deal of indifferent red wine has been downed for the sake of a bedside lamp.

There are fewer vineyards between here and handsome old Heidelberg, but much replanting is going on, and I look forward to some dry Baden wines from classic grapes being available for export.

Finally, an isolated corner of the Baden region up in the north, around Tauberbischofsheim, on the edge of Franconia, a countryside in which I have eaten the local snails, been eaten in my turn by the local mosquitoes, and assuaged my thirst from the only German wine other than those of Franconia and those few from near Baden-Baden, mentioned above, allowed to be sold in bottles the shape of a billy-goat's scrotum.

THE VINEYARDS OF BADEN

BADISCHES FRANKENLAND (*Bereich*)

TAUBERKLINGE: *Grosslage*

Weinbauort (*village*)	Einzellage (*vineyard*)
Beckstein	Kirchberg
	Nonnenberg
Boxberg (Stadtteil Unterschüpf)	Mühlberg
Dertingen	Mandelberg
	Sonnenberg
Gerlachsheim	Herrenberg
Grossrinderfeld	Beilberg
Höhefeld	Kemelrain
Kembach	Sonnenberg
Königheim	Kirchberg
Königshofen	Kirchberg
	Turmberg
	Walterstal
Krautheim	Heiligenberg
Krautheim (Stadtteil Klepsau)	Heiligenberg
Külsheim	Hoher Herrgott
Lauda	Altenberg
	Frankenberg
	Nonnenberg
Lindelbach	Ebenrain
Marbach	Frankenberg
Oberlauda	Altenberg
	Steinklinge
Oberschüpf	Altenberg
	Herrenberg
Reicholzheim	First
	Kemelrain
	Satzenberg

Weinbauort (village)	Einzellage (vineyard)
Sachsenflur	Kailberg
Tauberbischofsheim	Edelberg
Tauberbischofsheim (Ortsteil Impfingen)	Silberquell
Uissigheim	Stahlberg
Werbach	Beilberg
	Hirschberg
Wertheim	Schlossberg

BADISCHE BERGSTRASSE / KRAICHGAU (Bereich)

HOHENBERG: Grosslage

Berghausen	Sonnenberg
Bilfingen	Klepberg
Dietlingen	Keulebuckel
	Klepberg
Dürrn	Eichelberg
Eisingen	Klepberg
	Steig
Ellmendingen	Keulebuckel
Ersingen	Klepberg
Grötzingen	Lichtenberg
	Turmberg
Hohenwettersbach	Rosengarten
Karlsruhe-Durlach	Turmberg
Söllingen	Rotenbusch
Walzbachtal (Ortsteil Jöhlingen)	Hasensprung
Wcingarten	Katzenberg
	Petersberg
Wöschbach	Steinwengert

MANNABERG: Grosslage

Bad Mingolsheim-Langenbrücken, Ortsteil Bad Langenbrücken, Ortsteil Bad Mingolsheim	Goldberg
Bruchsal (Stadtteil Obergrombach)	Burgwingert
Bruchsal	Klosterberg

Weinbauort (village)	*Einzellage (vineyard)*
Bruchsal (Stadtteil Untergrombach)	Michaelsberg
	Weinhecke
Dielheim	Rosenberg
	Teufelskopf
Heidelberg	Burg
	Dachsbuckel
	Herrenberg
Heidelsheim	Altenberg
Helmsheim	Burgwingert
Horrenberg	Osterberg
Kraichtal (Stadtteil Oberöwisheim, Stadtteil Unteröwisheim)	Kirchberg
Leimen	Herrenberg
	Kreuzweg
Malsch	Ölbaum
	Rotsteig
Malschenberg	Ölbaum
Mühlhausen	Heiligenstein
Nussloch	Wilhelmsberg
Östringen	Hummelberg
	Rosenkranzweg
	Ulrichsberg
Rauenberg	Burggraf
Rettigheim	Ölbaum
Rotenberg	Schlossberg
Tairnbach	Rosenberg
Ubstadt-Weiher (Ortsteil Stettfeld)	Himmelreich
Ubstadt-Weiher (Ortsteil Ubstadt)	Weinhecke
Wiesloch	Bergwäldle
	Hägenich
	Spitzenberg
Zeutern	Himmelreich

RITTERSBERG: *Grosslage*

Dossenheim	Ölberg
Grossachsen	Sandrocken

Weinbauort (village)	Einzellage (vineyard)
Heidelberg	Heiligenberg
	Sonnenseite ob der Bruck
Hemsbach	Herrnwingert
Hohensachsen	Stephansberg
Laudenbach	Sonnberg
Leutershausen	Kahlberg
	Staudenberg
Lützelsachsen	Stephansberg
Schriesheim	Kuhberg
	Madonnenberg
	Schlossberg
	Staudenberg
Sulzbach	Herrnwingert
Weinheim	Hubberg
	Wüstberg

STIFTSBERG: *Grosslage*

Bauerbach	Lerchenberg
Binau	Herzogsberg
Diedesheim	Herzogsberg
Eberbach	Schollerbuckel
Eichelberg	Kapellenberg
Eichtersheim	Sonnenberg
Elsenz	Spiegelberg
Eppingen	Lerchenberg
Eschelbach	Sonnenberg
Flehingen	Lerchenberg
Gemmingen	Vogelsang
Hassmersheim	Kirchweinberg
Heinsheim	Burg Ehrenberg
Herbolzheim	Berg
Kirchardt (Ortsteil Berwangen)	Vogelsang
Kraichtal (Stadtteil Bahnbrücken, Stadtteil Gochsheim, Stadtteil Oberacker)	Lerchenberg

Weinbauort (village)	*Einzellage (vineyard)*
Kraichtal (Stadtteil Neuenbürg, Stadtteil Menzingen, Stadtteil Münzesheim)	Silberberg
Kraichtal (Stadtteil Landshausen, Stadtteil Menzingen)	Spiegelberg
Kürnbach	Lerchenberg
Michelfeld	Himmelberg
	Sonnenberg
Mühlbach	Lerchenberg
Neckarmühlbach	Hohberg
Neckarzimmern	Götzhalde
	Kirchweinberg
	Wallmauer
Neudenau	Berg
Odenheim	Königsbecher
Rohrbach a. G.	Lerchenberg
Sinsheim (Stadtteil Hilsbach)	Eichelberg
Sinsheim (Stadtteil Weiler)	Goldberg
	Steinsberg
Steinsfurt	Steinsberg
Sulzfeld	Burg Ravensburger Dicker Franz
	Burg Ravensburger Husarenkappe
	Burg Ravensburger Löchle
	Lerchenberg
Tiefenbach	Schellenbrunnen
	Spiegelberg
Waldangelloch	Sonnenberg
Zaisenhausen	Lerchenberg

BREISGAU (*Bereich*)

BURG LICHTENECK: *Grosslage*

Weinbauort (village)	Einzellage (vineyard)
Altdorf	Kaiserberg
Bleichheim	Kaiserberg
Bombach	Sommerhalde
Broggingen	Kaiserberg
Ettenheim	Kaiserberg
Hecklingen	Schlossberg
Heimbach	Bieninberg
Herbolzheim	Kaiserberg
Kenzingen	Hummelberg
	Roter Berg
Köndringen	Alte Burg
Malterdingen	Bienenberg
Mundingen	Alte Burg
Nordweil	Herrenberg
Ringsheim	Kaiserberg
Tutschfelden	Kaiserberg
Wagenstadt	Hummelberg

BURG ZÄHRINGEN: *Grosslage*

Buchholz	Sonnhalde
Denzlingen	Eichberg
	Sonnhalde
Emmendingen (Ortsteil Hochburg)	Halde
Freiburg i. Br. (Ortsteil Lehen)	Bergle
	Schlossberg
Glottertal	Eichberg
	Roter Bur
Heuweiler	Eichberg
Sexau	Sonnhalde
Wildtal	Sonnenberg

SCHUTTERLINDENBERG: *Grosslage*

Weinbauort (village)	Einzellage (vineyard)
Ettenheim (Ortsteil Wallburg)	Kirchberg
Friesenheim	Kronenbühl
Heiligenzell	Kronenbühl
Hugsweier	Kronenbühl
Kippenheim	Haselstaude
Lahr	Herrentisch
	Kronenbühl
Mahlberg	Haselstaude
Mietersheim	Kronenbühl
Münchweiler	Kirchberg
Oberschopfheim	Kronenbühl
Oberweier	Kronenbühl
Schmieheim	Kirchberg
Sulz	Haselstaude

BODENSEE (*Bereich*)

SONNENUFER: *Grosslage*

Bermatingen	Leopoldsberg
Bodman	Königsweingarten
Hagnau	Burgstall
Hilzingen	Elisabethenberg
Immenstaad	Burgstall
Kippenhausen	Burgstall
Konstanz	Sonnenhalde
Markdorf	Burgstall
	Sängerhalde
Meersburg	Bengel
	Chorherrnhalde
	Fohrenberg
	Haltnau
	Jungfernstieg
	Lerchenberg
	Rieschen

Weinbauort (village)	Einzellage (vineyard)
Meersburg	Sängerhalde
Oberuhldingen	Kirchhalde
Reichenau	Hochwart
Salem (Ortsteil Kirchberg)	Schlossberg
Singen	Elisabethenberg
	Olgaberg
Stetten	Fohrenberg
	Lerchenberg
	Sängerhalde
Überlingen	Felsengarten

Not yet assigned a Grosslage:

Klettgau (Ortsteil Erzingen)	Kapellenberg
Klettgau (Ortsteil Rechberg)	Kapellenberg
Lottstetten (Ortsteil Nack)	Steinler

KAISERSTUHL-TUNIBERG (Bereich)

ATTILAFELSEN: Grosslage

Gottenheim	Kirchberg
Merdingen	Bühl
Munzingen	Kapellenberg
Niederrimsingen	Rotgrund
Oberrimsingen	Franziskaner
Opfingen	Sonnenberg
Tiengen	Rebtal
Waltershofen	Steinmauer

VULKANFELSEN: Grosslage

Achkarren	Castellberg
	Schlossberg
Amoltern	Steinhalde
Bahlingen	Silberberg
Bickensohl	Herrenstück
	Steinfelsen
Bischoffingen	Enselberg

Weinbauort (village)	Einzellage (vineyard)
Bischoffingen	Rosenkranz
	Steinbuck
Bötzingen	Eckberg
	Lasenberg
Breisach a. Rh.	Augustinerberg
	Eckartsberg
Burkheim	Feuerberg
	Schlossgarten
Eichstetten	Herrenbuck
	Lerchenberg
Endingen	Engelsberg
	Steingrube
	Tannacker
Ihringen	Castellberg
	Fohrenberg
	Kreuzhalde
	Schlossberg
	Steinfelsen
	Winklerberg
Ihringen (Ortsteil Blankenhornsberg)	Doktorgarten
Jechtingen	Eichert.
	Enselberg
	Gestühl
	Hochberg
	Steingrube
Kiechlinsbergen	Ölberg
	Teufelsburg
Königschaffhausen	Hasenberg
	Steingrüble
Leiselheim	Gestühl
Neuershausen	Steingrube
Nimburg	Steingrube
Oberbergen	Bassgeige
	Pulverbuck
Oberrotweil	Eichberg
	Henkenberg

Weinbauort (village)	*Einzellage (vineyard)*
Oberrotweil	Käsleberg
	Kirchberg
	Schlossberg
Riegel	St Michaelsberg
Sasbach	Limburg
	Lützelberg
	Rote Halde
	Scheibenbuck
Schelingen	Kirchberg
Wasenweiler	Kreuzhalde
	Lotberg

MARKGRÄFLERLAND (*Bereich*)

BURG NEUENFELS: *Grosslage*

Auggen	Letten
	Schäf
Bad Bellingen	Sonnenstück
Badenweiler	Römerberg
Ballrechten-Dottingen	Altenberg
	Castellberg
Britzingen	Altenberg
	Rosenberg
	Sonnhohle
Britzingen (Ortsteil Dattingen)	Altenberg
	Rosenberg
	Sonnhohle
Feldberg	Paradies
Hügelheim	Gottesacker
	Höllberg
	Schlossgarten
Laufen	Altenberg
Liel	Sonnenstück
Lipburg	Kirchberg
Mauchen	Frauenberg
	Sonnenstück

Weinbauort (village)	Einzellage (vineyard)
Müllheim	Pfaffenstück
	Reggenhag
	Sonnhalde
Niedereggenen	Röthen
	Sonnenstück
Niederweiler	Römerberg
Obereggenen	Röthen
Schliengen	Sonnenstück
Steinenstadt	Schäf
	Sonnenstück
Sulzburg	Altenberg
Zunzingen	Rosenberg

LORETTOBERG: *Grosslage*

Bad Krotzingen	Steingrüble
Biengen	Maltesergarten
Bollschweil	Steinberg
Buggingen	Höllberg
	Maltesergarten
Ebringen	Sommerberg
Ehrenstetten	Oelberg
	Rosenberg
Eschbach	Maltesergarten
Freiburg i. Br.	Jesuitenschloss
	Steinler
Grunern	Altenberg
	Schlossberg
Heitersheim	Maltesergarten
	Sonnhohle
Kirchhofen	Batzenberg
	Höllhagen
	Kirchberg
Mengen	Alemannenbuck
Merzhausen	Jesuitenschloss
Norsingen	Batzenberg
Pfaffenweiler	Batzenberg

Weinbauort (village)	*Einzellage (vineyard)*
Pfaffenweiler	Oberdürrenberg
Schallstadt-Wolfenweile	Batzenberg
	Dürrenberg
Scherzingen	Batzenberg
Schlatt	Maltesergarten
	Steingrüble
Seefelden	Maltesergarten
Staufen	Schlossberg
Staufen (Ortsteil Wettelbrunn)	Maltesergarten
Tunsel	Maltesergarten
Wittnau	Kapuzinerbuck

VOGTEI RÖTTELN: *Grosslage*

Bamlach	Kapellenberg
Binzen	Sonnhohle
Blansingen	Wolfer
Efringen-Kirchen	Kirchberg
	Oelberg
	Sonnhohle
	Steingässle
Egringen	Sonnhohle
Eimeldingen	Sonnhohle
Feuerbach	Steingässle
Fischingen	Sonnhohle
Grenzach	Hornfelsen
Haltingen	Stiege
Herten	Steinacker
Hertingen	Sonnhohle
Holzen	Steingässle
Huttingen	Kirchberg
Istein	Kirchberg
Kleinkems	Wolfer
Lörrach	Sonnenbrunnen
Ötlingen	Sonnhohle
	Stiege
Rheinweiler	Kapellenberg

Weinbauort (village)	*Einzellage (vineyard)*
Riedlingen	Steingässle
Rümmingen	Sonnhohle
Schallbach	Sonnhohle
Tannenkirch	Steingässle
Weil am Rhein	Schlipf
	Stiege
Welmlingen	Steingässle
Wintersweiler	Steingässle
Wollbach	Steingässle

ORTENAU (*Bereich*)

FÜRSTENECK: *Grosslage*

Berghaupten	Kinzigtäler
Bermersbach	Kinzigtäler
Bottenau	Renchtäler
Diersburg	Kinzigtäler
	Schlossberg
Durbach	Bienengarten
	Josephsberg
	Kapellenberg
	Kasselberg
	Kochberg
	Ölberg
	Plauelrain
	Schlossberg
	Schloss Grohl
	Steinberg
Erlach	Renchtäler
Gengenbach	Kinzigtäler
	Nollenköpfle
Hofweier	Kinzigtäler
Lautenbach	Renchtäler
Nesselried	Renchtäler
	Schlossberg
Niederschopfheim	Kinzigtäler

Weinbauort (village)	Einzellage (vineyard)
Nussbach	Renchtäler
Offenburg (Ortsteil Zell-Weierbach)	Abtsberg
Offenburg (Ortsteil Fessenbach)	Bergle
	Franzensberger
Oberkirch	Renchtäler
Oberkirch (Ortsteil Haslach)	Renchtäler
Ödsbach	Renchtäler
Ohlsbach	Kinzigtäler
Ortenberg	Andreasberg
	Franzensberger
	Freudental
	Schlossberg
Rammersweier	Kreuzberg
Reichenbach	Amselberg
	Kinzigtäler
Ringelbach	Renchtäler
Stadelhofen	Renchtäler
Tiergarten	Renchtäler
Ulm	Renchtäler
Zunsweier	Kinzigtäler

SCHLOSS RODECK: *Grosslage*

Achern (Ortsteil Oberachern)	Alter Gott
	Bienenberg
Altschweier	Sternenberg
Baden-Baden	Eckberg
	Sätzler
Bühl (Ortsteil Neusatz)	Burg Windeck
	Kastanienhalde
	Sternenberg
	Wolfhag
Bühlertal	Engelsfelsen
	Klotzberg
Eisental	Betschgräbler
	Sommerhalde
Kappelrodeck	Hex vom Dasenstein

Weinbauort (village)	*Einzellage (vineyard)*
Lauf	Alter Gott
	Gut Alsenhof
	Schloss Neu-Windeck
Mösbach	Kreuzberg
Neuweier	Altenberg
	Gänsberg
	Heiligenstein
	Mauerberg
	Schlossberg
Obersasbach	Alter Gott
	Eichwäldele
Obertsrot	Grafensprung
Ottersweier	Althof
	Wolfhag
Renchen	Kreuzberg
Sasbachwalden	Alter Gott
	Klostergut Schelzberg
Sinzheim	Frühmessler
	Fremersberger Feigenwäldchen
	Klostergut
	Sätzler
	Sonnenberg
Steinbach	Stich den Buben
	Yburgberg
Varnhalt	Klosterbergfelsen
	Sonnenberg
	Steingrübler
Waldulm	Kreuzberg
	Pfarrberg
Weisenbach	Kestelberg

Württemburg

0   15 miles

0   25km

N

Tauber

Bad Mergentheim

Neckar

Jagdst

Kocher

Gundelsheim   Künzelsau

Heilbronn   Weinsberg

Brackenheim

Bönnigheim   Grossbottwar

Maulbronn

Illingen   Beitigheim

Vaihingen   *Murr*

Ludwigsburg

Waiblingen   *Rems*

Bad Cannstadt

Stuttgart   Schnait

Esslingen

Neckar

CHAPTER 15

Württemberg

Area:	6,295 hectares
Average crop:	460,000 hectolitres
Types:	53 per cent red
	47 per cent white
Vines:	26 per cent Trollinger
	22 per cent Riesling
	10 per cent Spätburgunder
	14 per cent Silvaner
	11 per cent Portugieser
	6 per cent Müller-Thurgau
	6 per cent Limberger

Württemberg is a region of small growers (many of them, indeed, part-time growers), and therefore of big cooperatives – a region of vineyards scattered rather than spread chiefly over the middle and lower reaches of the Neckar, and its tributaries.

It is separated from its western neighbour, Baden, by the high tops of the Black Forest, and from Franconia, to the north, by the heights of the Taubergrund.

But if it is a region of small growers, it is a region of big drinkers: it has been estimated that Württembergers drink four times as much as they grow – much of it red wine imported largely from France and from Italy.

It grows red wine, too – more red than white: the Limberger gives a softer, blander wine than the bigger-bodied wine of the bigger Trollinger grape. The best of the reds are, as elsewhere, the Spätburgunder.

The reason for the wide variety is not only the smallness of the holdings but also the sturdy individuality of the growers, each positive that he knows best what grape to grow, and how to grow it.

He is probably right. Württemberg weather is violently changeable – more of an extreme continental climate than its neighbours on the Rhine, and subject to storms and sudden frosts because of the clash between warm air from the west and the cold air of the continental land-mass.

This means that there is a wide variety of micro-climates: this patch of land in its river valley is sheltered from the wind, that one lies above the ground frosts of spring and autumn. Different varieties of grape will thrive, therefore, within quite short distances of each other according to climate and to soil.

Included in the statistics as red wine is the local speciality, *Schillerwein* (see page 62), a deep pink wine made by pressing together the grapes of red and white varieties grown higgledy-piggledy together in the same vineyard – a method of viti-culture not altogether smiled upon by authority, but widely produced and widely enjoyed throughout the region. (I have seen it stated that as much *Schillerwein* is produced as white and true red wine put together.)

The name derives not from that of the poet, but from the verb *schillern*, to shimmer or glitter. Note that the German wine law distinguishes between *Schillerwein*, permitting the name only to Württemberg QbA and QmP wines made in the way I have described, or from a light pressing of red grapes, and such other pink wines as the *Weissherbst* of Baden (see Chapter 5).

Considering the difficulties of the climate, and the problems that beset the small man – lack not only of capital but of access to special knowledge and of time to experiment – it is surprising that so much good wine is grown in Württemberg (and a matter of regret that little, if any, is exported, even to other regions of Germany). Some Württemberg Rieslings are particularly successful.

To a great extent this is because necessity has been made a virtue: small men need to cooperate, and cooperatives can afford modern equipment and experimental stations and vineyards.

So not only the Weinsberg Training and Research Institute, a state enterprise, near Heilbronn, but the Central State Association of Cooperatives at Stuttgart has done an immense amount to investigate the suitability of various types of vine to various soils and climates, to experiment with hybrids, with new methods of pest control and of vinification. The Association is also able to vinify, cellar and bottle, all under ideal conditions.

Cooperation in wine-production has gone a long way in Germany (see Chapter 1) but cooperation on this scale – to the extent that one single cooperative in Stuttgart is said to handle wine from an acreage three times that of the whole Rheingau – is especially impressive in a region where – it was a Württemberger who told me – the locals will sit for an hour or more over a litre of wine apiece without exchanging a word until one will up and say 'enough of this chit-chat: time to be getting home'.

THE VINEYARDS OF WÜRTTEMBERG

KOCHER-JAGST-TAUBER (*Bereich*)

KOCHERBERG: *Grosslage*

Weinbauort (*village*)	*Einzellage* (*vineyard*)
Belsenberg	Heilig Kreuz
Bieringen	Schlüsselberg

Weinbauort (village)	Einzellage (vineyard)
Criesbach	Burgstall
	Hoher Berg
	Sommerberg
Dörzbach	Altenberg
Ernsbach	Flatterberg
Forchtenberg	Flatterberg
Ingelfingen	Hoher Berg
Künzelsau	Hoher Berg
Möckmühl	Ammerlanden
	Hofberg
Niedernhall	Burgstall
	Engweg
	Hoher Berg
Siglingen	Hofberg
Weissbach	Altenberg
	Engweg
Widdern	Hofberg

TAUBERBERG: *Grosslage*

Elpersheim	Mönchsberg
	Probstberg
Wermutshausen	Schafsteige

Not yet assigned a *Grosslage* :

Kressbronn am Bodensee	Berghalde
Tübingen (Ortsteile Hirschau, Unterjesingen)	Sonnenhalden
Haagen	Schafsteige
Laudenbach	Schafsteige
Markelsheim	Mönchsberg
	Probstberg
Niederstetten	Schafsteige
Oberstetten	Schafsteige
Reinsbronn	Röde
Vorbachzimmern	Schafsteige
Weikersheim	Hardt

Weinbauort (village)	*Einzellage (vineyard)*
Weikersheim	Karlsberg
	Schmecker

REMSTAL-STUTTGART (*Bereich*)

HOHENNEUFFEN: *Grosslage*

Beuren	Schlossteige
Frickenhausen	Schlossteige
Kappishäusern	Schlossteige
Kohlberg	Schlossteige
Linsenhofen	Schlossteige
Metzingen	Hofsteige
	Schlossteige
Neuffen	Schlossteige
Weilheim	Schlossteige

KOPF: *Grosslage*

Beinstein	Grossmulde
Breuningsweiler	Holzenberg
Bürg	Schlossberg
Grossheppach	Wanne
Grunbach	Berghalde
Hanweiler	Berg
Kleinheppach	Greiner
Korb	Berg
	Hörnle
	Sommerhalde
Neustadt	Söhrenberg
Schorndorf	Grafenberg
Waiblingen	Hörnle
Winnenden	Berg
	Holzenberg
	Rossberg
Winterbach	Hungerberg

SONNENBÜHL: *Grosslage*

Weinbauort (village)	*Einzellage (vineyard)*
Beutelsbach	
Schnait i. R.	Burghalde
Endersbach	Hintere Klinge
Rommelshausen	
Stetten i. R.	Mönchhalde
Strümpfelbach	Altenberg

WARTBÜHL: *Grosslage*

Aichelberg	Luginsland
Baach	Himmelreich
Beutelsbach	Altenberg
	Käppele
	Sonnenberg
Breuningsweiler	Haselstein
Endersbach	Happenhalde
	Wetzstein
Geradstetten	Lichtenberg
	Sonnenberg
Grossheppach	Steingrüble
	Zügernberg
Grunbach	Klingle
Hanweiler	Maien
Hebsack	Lichtenberg
Hertmannsweiler	Himmelreich
Kleinheppach	Sonnenberg
	Steingrüble
Korb	Steingrüble
Rommelshausen	Häder
Schnait i. R.	Altenberg
	Sonnenberg
Stetten i. R.	Brotwasser
	Häder
	Lindhälder

Weinbauort (village)	*Einzellage (vineyard)*
Stetten i. R.	Puvermächer
Strümpfelbach	Gastenklinge
	Nonnenberg
Waiblingen	Steingrüble
Winnenden	Haselstein

WEINSTEIGE: *Grosslage*

Esslingen	Ailenberg
	Kirchberg
	Lerchenberg
	Schenkenberg
Fellbach	Gips
	Goldberg
	Herzogenberg
	Hinterer Berg
	Lämmler
	Mönchberg
	Wetzstein
Gerlingen	Bopser
Stuttgart	Kriegsberg
	Mönchberg
(Ortsteil Gaisburg)	Abelsberg
(Ortsteil Untertürkheim)	Gips
(Ortsteil Uhlbach)	Götzenberg
(Ortsteil Obertürkheim)	Ailenberg
(Ortsteil Untertürkheim)	Altenberg
(Ortsteile Bad Cannstatt, Feuerbach, Münster, Wangen, Zuffenhausen)	Berg
(Ortsteil Bad Cannstatt)	Halde
(Ortsteile Bad Cannstatt, Untertürkheim)	Herzogenberg
(Ortsteil Obertürkheim)	Kirchberg
(Ortsteile Hedelfingen, Rohracker)	Lenzenberg
(Ortsteile Bad Cannstatt, Untertürkheim)	Mönchberg

Weinbauort (village)	*Einzellage (vineyard)*
Stuttgart (Ortsteil Degerloch)	Scharrenberg
(Ortsteile Rotenberg, Uhlbach, Untertürkheim)	Schlossberg
(Ortsteil Uhlbach)	Steingrube
(Ortsteile Bad Cannstatt, Mühlhausen, Münster)	Steinhalde
(Ortsteil Untertürkheim)	Wetzstein
(Ortsteile Bad Cannstatt, Hofen, Mühlhausen, Münster)	Zuckerle

WÜRTTEMBERGISCH UNTERLAND (*Bereich*)

HEUCHELBERG: *Grosslage*

Brackenheim	Dachsberg
	Mönchsberg
	Schlossberg
	Wolfsaugen
	Zweifelberg
(Ortsteil Botenheim)	Ochsenberg
Burgbronn	Hahnenberg
Cleebronn	Michaelsberg
Dürrenzimmern	Mönchsberg
Eibensbach	Michaelsberg
Frauenzimmern	Kaiserberg
	Michaelsberg
Güglingen	Kaiserberg
	Michaelsberg
Haberschlacht	Dachsberg
Hausen/Z.	Jupiterberg
	Staig
	Vogelsang
Heilbronn (Ortsteil Klingenberg)	Schlossberg
	Sonntagsberg
Kleingartach	Grafenberg
	Vogelsang
Leingarten	Grafenberg

Weinbauort (village)	Einzellage (vineyard)
Leingarten	Leiersberg
	Vogelsang
Massenbachhausen	Krähenberg
Meimsheim	Katzenöhrle
Neipperg	Grafenberg
	Schlossberg
	Steingrube
	Vogelsang
Niederhofen	Grafenberg
	Vogelsang
Nordhausen	Sonntagsberg
Nordheim	Grafenberg
	Gräfenberg
	Ruthe
	Sonntagsberg
Pfaffenhofen	Hohenberg
Schwaigern	Grafenberg
	Ruthe
	Sonnenberg
	Vogelsang
Stetten a. H.	Sonnenberg
Stockheim	Altenberg
Weiler/Z.	Hohenberg
Zaberfeld	Hohenberg

KIRCHENWEINBERG: *Grosslage*

Flein	Altenberg
	Eselsberg
	Sonnenberg
Heilbronn	Altenberg
	Sonnenberg
Ilsfeld (Ortsteil Schozach)	Mühlberg
	Roter Berg
	Schelmenklinge
Lauffen	Jungfer
	Katzenbeisser

Weinbauort (village)	*Einzellage (vineyard)*
Lauffen	Nonnenberg
	Riedersbückele
Neckarwestheim	Herrlesberg
Talheim	Hohe Eiche
	Schlossberg
	Sonnenberg
Untergruppenbach	Schlossberg

LINDELBERG: *Grosslage*

Adolzfurt	Schneckenhof
Bretzfeld	Goldberg
Dimbach	Schlossberg
Eschelbach	Schwobajörgle
Geddelsbach	Schneckenhof
Harsberg (Ortsteil Neuholz)	Dachsteiger
	Spielbühl
Kesselfeld	Schwobajörgle
Langenbeutingen	Himmelreich
Maienfels	Schneckenhof
Michelbach a. W.	Dachsteiger
	Margarete
Obersöllbach	Margarete
Pfedelbach	Goldberg
Siebeneich	Himmelreich
	Schlossberg
Schwabbach	Schlossberg
Unterheimbach	Schneckenhof
Untersteinbach	Dachsteiger
Verrenberg	Goldberg
	Verenberg
Waldbach	Schlossberg
Windischenbach	Goldberg

SALZBERG: *Grosslage*

Affaltrach	Dieblesberg
	Zeilberg

Weinbauort (village)	Einzellage (vineyard)
Eberstadt	Dezberg
	Eberfürst
	Sommerhalde
Eichelberg	Hundsberg
Ellhofen	Altenberg
	Althälde
	Ranzenberg
Eschenau	Paradies
Gellmersbach	Dezberg
Grantschen	Wildenberg
Lehrensteinsfeld	Althälde
	Frauenzimmer
	Steinacker
Löwenstein	Altenberg
	Nonnenrain
	Wohlfahrtsberg
Löwenstein (Ortsteil Hösslinsülz)	Dieblesberg
	Zeilberg
Sülzbach	Altenberg
Weiler/Weinsberg	Hundsberg
	Schlierbach
Weinsberg	Althälde
	Ranzenberg
	Schemelsberg
Willsbach	Dieblesberg
	Zeilberg
Wimmental	Altenberg

SCHALKSTEIN: *Grosslage*

Affalterbach	Neckarhälde
Allmersbach a. W.	Alter Berg
Asperg	Berg
Beihingen	Neckarhälde
Benningen	Neckarhälde
Besigheim	Felsengarten
	Katzenöhrle

Weinbauort (village)	*Einzellage (vineyard)*
Besigheim	Neckarberg
	Wurmberg
Bietigheim	Neckarberg
Bissingen	Neckarberg
Erdmannhausen	Neckarhälde
Gemmrigheim	Neckarberg
	Wurmberg
Grossingersheim	Schlossberg
Hessigheim	Felsengarten
	Käsberg
	Katzenöhrle
Höpfigheim	Königsberg
Kirchberg	Kelterberg
Kleinaspach	Kelterberg
Kleiningersheim	Schlossberg
Löchgau	Neckarberg
Ludwigsburg (Ortsteil Hoheneck)	Neckarhälde
Marbach	Neckarhälde
Markgröningen	Berg
	Sankt Johännser
Mundelsheim	Käsberg
	Katzenöhrle
	Mühlbächer
	Rozenberg
Murr	Neckarhälde
Neckarweihingen	Neckarhälde
Poppenweiler	Neckarhälde
Rielinghausen	Kelterberg
Rietenau	Güldenkern
Steinheim/Murr	Burgberg
Walheim	Neckarberg
	Wurmberg

SCHOZACHTAL: *Grosslage*

Abstatt	Burgberg
	Burg Wildeck

Weinbauort (village)	Einzellage (vineyard)
Abstatt	Sommerberg
Auenstein	Burgberg
	Schlossberg
Ilsfeld	Rappen
Löwenstein	Sommerberg
Unterheinriet	Sommerberg

STAUFENBERG: *Grosslage*

Brettach	Berg
Cleversulzbach	Berg
Duttenberg	Schön
Erlenbach	Kayberg
Gundelsheim	Himmelreich
Heilbronn	Stahlbühl
	Stiftsberg
	Wartberg
Horkheim	Stiftsberg
Neckarsulm	Scheuerberg
Oedheim	Kayberg
Offenau	Schön
Talheim	Stiftsberg
Untereisesheim	Vogelsang

STROMBERG: *Grosslage*

Bönnigheim	Kirchberg
	Sonnenberg
Diefenbach	König
Ensingen	Schanzreiter
Erligheim	Lerchenberg
Freudenstein	Reichshalde
Freudental	Kirchberg
Gründelbach	Steinbachhof
	Wachtkopf
Häfnerhaslach	Heiligenberg
Hofen	Lerchenberg
Hohenhaslach	Kirchberg

Weinbauort (village)	Einzellage (vineyard)
Hohenhaslach	Klosterberg
Hohenstein	Kirchberg
Horrheim	Klosterberg
Illingen	Forstgrube
	Halde
	Lichtenberg
	Schanzreiter
Kirchheim	Kirchberg
Kleinsachsenheim	Kirchberg
Knittlingen	Reichshalde
Lienzingen	Eichelberg
Maulbronn	Eilfingerberg Klosterstück
	Reichshalde
Mühlhausen	Halde
Obererdingen	Kupferhalde
Ochsenbach	Liebenberg
Ötisheim	Sauberg
Riet	Kirchberg
Rosswag	Forstgrube
	Halde
	Lichtenberg
Schützingen	Heiligenberg
Spielberg	Liebenberg
Sternenfels	König
Vaihingen	Höllisch Feuer

WUNNENSTEIN: *Grosslage*

Beilstein	Schlosswengert
	Steinberg
	Wartberg
Gronau	Forstberg
Grossbottwar	Harzberg
	Lichtenberg
Hof und Lembach	Harzberg
	Lichtenberg
Ilsfeld	Lichtenberg

Weinbauort (village)	Einzellage (vineyard)
Kleinbottwar	Götzenberg
	Lichtenberg
	Oberer Berg
	Süssmund
Ludwigsburg (Ortsteil Hoheneck)	Oberer Berg
Oberstenfeld	Forstberg
	Harzberg
	Lichtenberg
Steinheim	Lichtenberg
Winzerhausen	Harzberg
	Lichtenberg

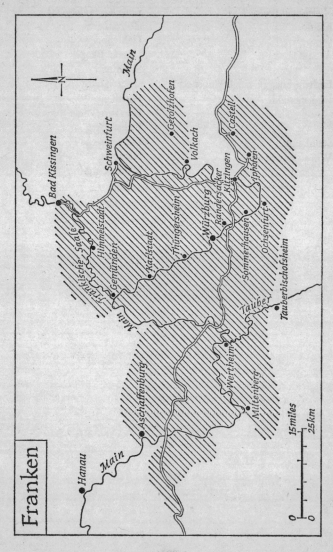

Franken

Hanau · Main · Aschaffenburg · Miltenberg · Wertheim · Tauberbischofsheim · Tauber · Ochsenfurt · Sommerhausen · Randersacker · Würzburg · Kitzingen · Iphofen · Castell · Volkach · Gerolzhofen · Schweinfurt · Thüngersheim · Karlstadt · Gemünden · Himmelstadt · Fränkische Saale · Bad Kissingen · Main

15 miles
25 km

CHAPTER 16

Franken

Area:	3,059 hectares
Average crop:	120,000 hectolitres
Types:	98 per cent white
	2 per cent red
Vines:	46 per cent Silvaner
	41 per cent Müller-Thurgau
	4 per cent Riesling

Politically, socially and economically, the river Main divides Germany into north and south.

Although many Franconian wines come from north of the river, around and beyond the city of Würzburg, this too is where in terms of wine the south begins.

Franconia is a small region and, because of its wayward and extreme continental-type climate, production is low even for its size. But its wines are of especial interest, especially to those who find the classic wines of the Rhine and the Mosel too sweet and flowery for drinking with meals: they are mostly dry, with a firm, full flavour.

Indeed, many British amateurs of wine admire them for the very reasons that made the American Frank Schoonmaker so half-hearted about them. After commenting on what he called 'almost a cult' for them, he went on:

I must admit that I cannot altogether share this boundless enthusiasm for wines which are almost always agreeable but hardly ever great, nor can I explain Goethe's preference for them except to say that they go very well with food, have a less pronounced bouquet and character than other German wines, are generally quite full-bodied and dry without being tart, and possibly taste more like Alsatian wines or white Burgundies than like Moselles and Rheingaus.[1]

'Good for them', will say many a wine-bibber, and point out that wines that are full-bodied and dry without being tart, and rather like Alsatians and white burgundies, can hardly be said to lack character.

(The reference to Goethe is a reminder that he is said to have drunk something like a couple of litres of wine a day, preferably Franconian. It is perhaps significant that Herr Adolf Steinmann of the Prince of Castell's estate at Castell, in the east of the region, a devoted custodian of the Franconian tradition, told me that in his opinion Franconian wines are 'intellectuals' wines', and that he sells much of his yield to universities.)

Not that Franconian wines do not differ widely between themselves: there are wide variations of soil – notably in four regions, one of mixed clay and chalk, or gypsum, known as *Keuper*, one of shell-lime soil (*Muschelkalk*), one of sandstone (*Buntsandstein*) and one of a kind of slate (*Glimmerschiefer*).

Silvaner and Müller-Thurgau wines grown in one area will differ so much from the same wines grown in others that in many restaurant and other wine-lists in Franconia the kind of soil that a wine comes from is given in brackets as well as the comment on its character that is usual in lists elsewhere, as it might be *trocken*, dry; *herb*, one stage less dry, but not at all sweet; *mild*, mild or sweetish; and even such phrases as *füllig, herzhaft, fruchtig* – 'full-bodied, hearty, fruity'; to say nothing of such, to me, meaningless but imposing words as *ausdrucksvoll*, 'expressive'.

For a long time it has been the custom to refer to any wine

1. Schoonmaker, Frank, *German Wines*, London, Oldbourne, 1957.

presented in the characteristic Franconian flask-shaped *Bocksbeutel* as Steinwein, but this is incorrect and, indeed, illegal.[2] A Steinwein is one from vineyards on the rocky slopes of the Würzburger Stein, overlooking the city of Würzburg itself.

Würzburg is the home of two almshouses which, like the Hospices de Beaune, produce fine wines from their own vineyards – the Juliusspital and the Burgerspital. And the cellars of the splendid early eighteenth-century Residenz are the home and headquarters of the state domain, the biggest wine-grower in Franconia, and producing some of the finest wines.

The cellars themselves are the noblest I have seen – more magnificent than those of Mouton, because they are architecturally integrated into the handsome baroque building, with huge carved eighteenth-century casks still in use, and a carved press dating from 1720 standing in the place of honour like an altar in a cathedral. (Other fine pieces are to be found in the Mainfränkisches museum in the neighbouring Marienberg castle.)

The Bavarian state is the biggest single wine-grower in all Germany, with thirteen vineyards, two other great cellars, and a fine viticultural research station at Thüngersheim.

Some of the German wines I have most enjoyed have been state-domain wines tasted in the Residenz or with luncheon in its charming garden-restaurant. And it is typical of the wines of Franconia that at an official tasting in the same city, referred to on page 43, ten of the forty-two wines tasted for QbA status were officially *trocken*, which means dry enough for diabetics,[3] and none, not even a 1971 *Spätlese*, was at all sweet.

2. The *Bocksbeutel* is discussed on p. 170. In Franconia all wines with any pretensions to quality are put up in *Bocksbeutel*. Only the most ordinary and cheapest wines are sold in litre bottles of the conventional shape.

3. By German standards, that is, and subject to a doctor's approval.

It seems to me that there should be a bigger market in the United Kingdom for these admirable wines than they have yet secured, or even tried to secure.

THE VINEYARDS OF FRANKEN

BAYER. BODENSEE (*Bereich*)

Weinbauort (*village*)	*Einzellage* (*vineyard*)
Nonnenhorn	Seehalde
	Sonnenbüchel

MAINDREIECK (*Bereich*)

BURG: *Grosslage*

Hammelburg	Heroldsberg
	Trautlestal
Ramsthal	St Klausen
Saaleck	Schlossberg
Wirmsthal	Scheinberg

EWIG LEBEN: *Grosslage*

Randersacker	Marsberg
	Pfülben
	Sonnenstuhl
	Teufelskeller

HOFRAT: *Grosslage*

Buchbrunn	Heisser Stein
Kitzingen	Wilhelmsberg
Mainstockheim	Hofstück
Marktbreit	Sonnenberg
Repperndorf	Kaiser Karl
Segnitz	Pfaffensteig
	Zobelsberg

The German standard is four grammes of residual sugar per litre: the UK standard is only one gramme.

Weinbauort (village)	Einzellage (vineyard)
Sulzfeld	Cyriakusberg
	Maustal

HONIGBERG: *Grosslage*

Dettelbach	Berg-Rondell
	Sonnenleite

KIRCHBERG: *Grosslage*

Astheim	Karthäuser
Escherndorf	Berg
	Fürstenberg
	Lump
Fahr	residual vineyards
Köhler	residual vineyards
Krautheim	Sonnenleite
Neuses	Glatzen
Neusetz	residual vineyards
Nordheim	Kreuzberg
	Vögelein
Obereisenheim	Höll
Obervolkach	Landsknecht
Sommerach	Katzenkopf
	Rosenberg
Stammheim	Eselsberg
Untereisenheim	Sonnenberg
Volkach	Ratsherr
Wipfeld	Zehntgraf

RAVENSBURG: *Grosslage*

Erlabrunn	Weinsteig
Güntersleben	Sommerstuhl
Retzbach	Benediktusberg
Thüngersheim	Johannisberg
	Scharlachberg
Veitshöchheim	Wölflein

Not yet assigned a *Grosslage* :

Weinbauort (village)	*Einzellage (vineyard)*
Böttigheim	Wurmberg
Eibelstadt	Kapellenberg
	Mönchsleite
Erlenbach bei Marktheidenfeld	Krähenschnabel
Frankenwinheim	Rosenberg
Frickenhausen am Main	Fischer
	Kapellenberg
	Markgraf Babenberg
Hallburg	Schlossberg
Homburg	Edelfrau
	Kallmuth
Lengfurt	Alter Berg
	Oberrot
Randersacker	Dabug
Rimpar	Kobersberg
Röttingen	Feuerstein
Schweinfurt	Mainleite
	Peterstirn
Sommerhausen	Reifenstein
	Steinbach
Tauberrettersheim	Königin
Veitshöchheim	Sonnenschein
Würzburg	Abtsleite
	Innere Leiste
	Kirchberg
	Pfaffenberg
	Schlossberg
	Stein
	Stein/Harfe

ROSSTAL: *Grosslage*

Arnstein	residual vineyards
Eussenheim	First
Gambach	Kalbenstein

Weinbauort (village)	*Einzellage (vineyard)*
Gössenheim	Arnberg
Himmelstadt	Kelter
Karlburg	residual vineyards
Karlstadt	Im Stein
Laudenbach	residual vineyards
Mühlbach	residual vineyards
Retzstadt	Langenberg
Stetten	Stein

MAINVIERECK (*Bereich*)

HEILIGENTHAL: *Grosslage*

Grossostheim	Reischklingeberg
	Harstell
Wenigumstadt	residual vineyards

Not yet assigned a *Grosslage*:

Aschaffenburg	Pompejaner
Bürgstadt	Centgrafenberg
	Mainhölle
Dorfprozelten	Predigtstuhl
Engelsberg	Klostergarten
Erlenbach a. Main	Hochberg
Grossheubach	Bischofsberg
Grosswallstadt	Lützeltalerberg
Klingenberg	Hochberg
	Schlossberg
Kreuzwertheim	Kaffelstein
Michelbach	Apostelgarten
	Steinberg
Miltenberg	Steingrübler
Rück	Jesuitenberg
	Johannisberg
Wasserlos	Schlossberg

REUSCHBERG: *Grosslage*

Weinbauort *(village)*	Einzellage *(vineyard)*
Hörstein	Abtsberg

STEIGERWALD *(Bereich)*

BURGWEG: *Grosslage*

Iphofen	Julius-Echter-Berg
	Kalb
	Kronsberg
Markt Einersheim	Vogelsang
Possenheim	residual vineyards

HERRENBERG: *Grosslage*

Castell	Bausch
	Feuerbach
	Hohnart
	Kirchberg
	Kugelspiel
	Reitsteig
	Schlossberg
	Trautberg

KAPELLENBERG: *Grosslage*

Schmachtenberg	Eulengrund
Steinbach	Nonnenberg
Zeil	Kronberg
Ziegelanger	Ölschnabel

SCHILD: *Grosslage*

Abtswind	Altenberg
Castell	Bausch
	Kirchberg
Greuth	Bastel

SCHLOSSBERG: *Grosslage*

Weinbauort (village)	*Einzellage (vineyard)*
Grosslangheim	Kiliansberg
Rödelsee	Küchenmeister
	Schwanleite
Sickershausen	Storchenbrünnle
Wiesenbronn	Wachhügel

SCHLOSSTÜCK: *Grosslage*

Bullenheim	Paradies
Ergersheim	Altenberg
Frankenberg	Herrschaftsberg
Hüttenheim	Tannenberg
Ippesheim	Herrschaftsberg
Seinsheim	Hohenbühl
Weimersheim	Roter Berg

Not yet assigned a *Grosslage*:

Altmannsdorf	Sonnenwinkel
Handthal	Stollberg
Kammerforst	Teufel
Kleinlangheim	Wutschenberg
Martinsheim	Langenstein
Michelau i. Steigerwald	Vollburg
Oberschwarzach	Herrenberg
Zeil a. Main	Mönchshang

CHAPTER 17

Bottles and Glasses

The tall, slender, virtually shoulderless bottle is so firmly associated in our minds with the wines of Germany that one might suppose it to date from time immemorial.

Authorities seem more or less agreed, however, that it dates from no longer ago than the first half of the nineteenth century. Before that, according to Simon and Hallgarten,[1] hock and Mosel bottles were similar to those used for burgundy. I have discovered no explanation for what must have been a pretty rapid change.

The German bottle now is of 0·70 litre capacity, very similar to, but not quite so tall as, the Alsatian *flûte*. The distinction between the amber bottle for hock and the green for Mosel is nearly, but not quite, so hard and fast as some writers would have us believe: I recall having seen, many years ago, Rhine wine being served at a banquet in Bonn from green bottles (and making a fool of myself by pronouncing to my neighbour, in a know-all sort of way, that here came a *Moselwein*) but not, unfortunately, exactly what wine it was. It may well have been from the Palatinate, for Schoonmaker,[2] writing less than twenty years ago, stated flatly that Pfalz bottles were green, like those of Alsace. Or it may be that there was a shortage of brown bottles during, and for some years after, the war. The distinction has become firmer in recent years, and nowadays the only green bottles in

1. *The Great Wines of Germany*, London, McGraw-Hill, 1963.
2. *German Wines*, London, Oldbourne, 1957.

which one sees Rhine wines are litre-sized, for the cheaper wines.

The flattened-spheroid *Bocksbeutel* of Franconia and part of Baden (see pages 170, 205) has a longer history, and is said to derive, like the *fiasco* of Chianti, from the flask slung from a medieval saddle-bow.

German wine-glasses vary widely in shape and style, but there is one major distinction – the heavy, knobbed, thick-stemmed *Römer*, from which we derive our own word, rummer, is used in Germany only for serving cheap 'open', or carafe, wine. It generally holds a quarter-litre, and one calls for it as a *Viertel*.

At table, hocks, Mosel and Franconian wines are all served in one form or another of tall-stemmed glass with a fairly rounded bowl, almost always faceted. Generally, and not only in Germany but also in stylish British and American restaurants and clubs, the tradition is honoured of using brown-stemmed but clear-bowled glasses for hock, green-stemmed for Mosel.

Until recently the bowl, too, would have been coloured, probably with clear cutting. The colour was to conceal cloudiness, or unsightly flecks floating in the wine, but now that filtering has been perfected, and is universal, a coloured hock-glass is as unnecessarily Victorian a vulgarity as a fish-knife.

Myself, I dislike even the colourless hock-glass as being unaesthetically top-heavy, and dislike it even more if cut. I serve German wines in the same plain tulip-shaped, relatively short-stemmed, glass in which I serve all wines, French or German, red or white.

I have said that filtering has done away with the flecks that made coloured glasses desirable. But it does not do away with the crystals that sometimes form on the corks of German wine-bottles, or in suspension. These are formed by crystallization of various tartrates and, far from being harmful, they indicate that the grapes were fully ripe when picked, and that the wine has been aged enough.

*

German wine-lovers do not chill their wines quite so much as we do – cellar-cool is cold enough, and they are probably right. It is easy to numb the delicate fragrance and flavour of a German wine by too much chilling.

This, though, is not to decry the value of a refrigerator in keeping even the finest hocks or Mosels after their bottles have been opened.

Many years ago, in the course of a tour of the Rheingau with Fritz Hallgarten, I tasted fine *Beerenauslesen* and *Trockenbeerenauslesen* from bottles that had been opened a fortnight before, poured from, firmly recorked, and kept in a refrigerator at the firm's tasting-room in Oestrich. They were so good that it was impossible to suppose that any deterioration had taken place, and Dr Hallgarten assured me that they were as good as they had ever been.

More recently, in a letter to *The Times*, he wrote that the

contention that wine does not keep long in an opened bottle is out of date. Oxidization [sic] leads to deterioration, depending on quantity and time. Modern vinification successfully avoids contact with air during rackings and even bottling, therefore air after opening the bottle has little effect for quite a time. Since 1951 (see *Rhineland Wineland*) I have made intense research into this problem.

Conclusions: 1. *German wines* will increase in quality after opening of bottle for as many days as the wine needs years to reach full maturity. *Spätlesen* or *Auslesen* with five to seven years to maturity taste better on the fourth to sixth day than when newly uncorked. *Beeren, Trockenbeerenauslesen* keep for months in the same healthy state. Always keep wine in the original bottle, recork with a clean cork (important).

2. *Sparkling wine* will keep for weeks, as long as carbonic acid is

retained, therefore, after pouring, close bottle immediately and firmly.

3. *Storing in a refrigerator* with an approximate temperature of 6° C has no bad effect. Wine transport in Europe takes place during temperatures well below 6° C. Maturation of the wine may be held back, tartaric crystals (completely harmless) may be precipitated, but they only make the wine rounder and softer. A freezer would be deadly!

*

As for keeping unopened bottles of German wine, the tendency nowadays is to drink them perhaps younger than necessary, in our anxiety to capture that youthful freshness. I remember Otto Loeb telling me that even a modest Mosel – one not up to the *Spätlese* class – could take three years to lose its initial acidity and still be crisply refreshing.

Spätlese and *Auslese* wines of good years can stay at their peak for ten, or a dozen, or fifteen years, and the great dessert wines longer still – twenty years and more. Though we cannot hope that every vintage likely to come our way will match the 1727 Rüdesheimer from the Apostel cellar in Bremen Town Hall, which I referred to on page 28, I must now quote the tasting note made on 13 May 1973 by Mr Michael Broadbent, the head of Christie's wine department, on the bottle of the same year opened at Schloss Vollrads for Count Matushka-Greiffenclau's eightieth birthday:

Yellow-amber gold, not unlike old Tokay; gently maderized and nutty; very dry, deep madeira-like flavour with excellent life-preserving acidity.

A very rare experience.

Appendix
German Wine Production, by Region and Category 1973–5

Region	Vine area in production (Hectares)			Must production (Hectolitres)		
	1973	1974	1975*	1973	1974	1975*
Ahr	484	482	483	52,419	38,125	43,000
Baden	11,582	12,240	11,611	1,344,582	603,366	945,000
Franken	2,983	3,120	2,893	330,694	150,525	335,000
Hess. Bergstrasse	307	288	272	40,389	21,028	29,000
Mittelrhein	915	854	882	91,682	57,516	75,000
Mosel-Saar-Ruwer	11,258	11,525	11,369	1,645,682	1,128,745	1,385,000
Nahe	4,106	4,206	4,449	488,486	358,415	416,000
Rheingau	2,943	3,018	2,858	336,492	191,731	277,000
Rheinhessen	19,027	19,813	19,054	2,546,462	1,867,416	2,180,000
Rheinpfalz	19,823	20,217	19,574	2,847,147	2,025,330	2,200,000
Württemberg	7,194	7,264	7,493	972,765	363,094	710,000
Total	80,622	83,028	80,938	10,696,780†	6,805,291	8,595,000

* The figures for 1975 are approximate only.
† The 1973 vintage in Germany was the biggest on record.

Tafelwein (Hectolitres)			Qualitätswein (Hectolitres)			Prädikatswein (Hectolitres)		
1973	1974	1975*	1973	1974	1975*	1973	1974	1975*
1,271	3,130	860	28,217	23,836	14,620	22,931	11,159	27,520
8,405	23,234	Nil	442,174	317,966	283,500	874,003	262,166	661,500
2,058	16,225	Nil	221,940	118,070	147,400	76,696	16,230	187,600
356	3,031	Nil	31,913	16,584	17,400	8,100	1,413	11,600
1,747	8,651	10,500	57,244	39,538	10,500	32,691	9,327	54,000
5,055	233,471	13,850	858,232	697,417	332,400	572,395	197,857	1,038,750
3,520	25,650	Nil	302,847	246,196	120,640	177,119	86,569	295,360
6,062	18,665	11,080	199,803	143,340	102,490	130,627	29,726	163,430
9,127	82,631	Nil	1,675,384	1,323,215	872,000	790,951	461,570	1,308,000
7,273	119,562	66,000	1,980,342	1,401,278	968,000	734,532	504,490	1,166,000
7,097	9,867	Nil	697,016	300,421	497,000	262,652	52,806	213,000
9,971	544,117	102,290	6,495,122	4,627,861	3,365,950	3,682,697	1,633,313	5,126,760

Bibliography

For the historical background to the growing and drinking of German (and of other) wines, three books are essential:

Hyams, Edward, *Dionysus: A Social History of the Wine Vine*, London, Thames and Hudson, 1965.

Simon, André L., *The History of the Wine Trade in England*, London, Holland Press, 1964 (reissue).

Younger, William, *Gods, Men and Wine*, London, Michael Joseph, 1966.

I have also consulted, among others:

Henderson, Alexander, *The History of Ancient and Modern Wines*, London, 1824.

Johnson, Hugh, *Wine*, London, Mitchell Beazley, revised ed. 1974; *The World Atlas of Wine*, London, Mitchell Beazley, 1971.

Penzer, N. M., *The Book of the Wine-label*, London, Home & Van Thal, 1947.

Redding, Cyrus, *A History and Description of Modern Wines*, London, 1833; third edition, with additions and corrections, 1860.

Seltman, Charles, *Wine in the Ancient World*, London, Routledge & Kegan Paul, 1957.

Shand, Morton, *A Book of Wines Other than French*, London, Knopf, 1929.

Shaw, T. G., *Wine, the Vine and the Cellar*, London, Longman Green, 1863.

Until recently, the basic books on the German wines of our own time have been:

Hallgarten, S. F., *Rhineland Wineland*, 1951; 4th ed., London, Arlington Books, 1965.

Langenbach, Alfred, *German Wines and Vines*, London, Vista Books, 1962.

Schoonmaker, Frank, *German Wines*, London, Oldbourne, 1957.

with, lightweight though it is, in spite of its handsome outward aspect and the distinction of its joint authors:

Simon, André L., and Hallgarten, S. F., *The Great Wines of Germany*, London, McGraw-Hill, 1963.

Now, the German wine law of 1971 and other developments have made these to varying degrees out of date (though they are still of interest), and quite the most up-to-date, encyclopaedic and authoritative work is undoubtedly: Hallgarten, S. F., *German Wines*, London, Faber, 1976, which appeared when my own completed manuscript was already with the publishers, or I should have drawn heavily upon it – been tempted, indeed, to overdraw . . . This covers all the German regions: in the same splendid series, generally edited for Faber by Julian Jeffs, Q.C., is the only book to be devoted entirely to one region: Loeb, O. W., and Prittie, Terence, *Moselle*, London, Faber, 1972. These two apart, much comprehensive, scholarly and up-to-date information on German wines in general is to be found under the names of the respective regions in

Lichine, Alexis, *Encyclopaedia of Wines and Spirits*, London, Cassell, 1975. (It is important to consult this latest, revised, edition.)

General Index

Note Individual vineyards have not been indexed, as they can be found in the list of vineyards in the appropriate chapter.

220